MORE PRAISE FOR *A Natural Sense of Wonder*

"All parents, take note! In this enthusiastic and poetic drift of essays, Van Noy sets out to unveil the natural world for his children and finds himself on his own voyage of discovery. Walking
in the footsteps of Rachel Carson, who believed that nature provided young people an 'inner resource of strength' to last a life-
time, Van Noy seeks to imbue children with wonder. This book,
which moves at the delightful pace of a summer's day, is filled with
the passion of a good naturalist and the sensibilities of a loving
parent. Its motherlode chapter, 'Dirt World,' which offers advice
on how to get children outdoors, is worth the price of the book."
—Janisse Ray, author of *Ecology of a Cracker Childhood*

"'Here's something!' says Van Noy's daughter when she spots a
snail trail on their sidewalk, and her father pays attention. *A Natural Sense of Wonder* is filled with explorations of such 'ordinary
enchantments' too often lost in the swirl of our hyperscheduled
lives. Van Noy treats his children and his readers with warmth
and respect, seamlessly squeezing a good deal of natural history,
etymology, and literary savvy into his stories of snot-otters and
snake whisperers. He is a full participant in his family's home territory on Virginia's New River, and we can ask for no better re-
minder that 'every moment is a now' in our own home landscapes."
—Stephen Trimble, coauthor of *The Geography of Childhood: Why
Children Need Wild Places*

a natural
sense of wonder

THE UNIVERSITY OF GEORGIA PRESS ✳ ATHENS AND LONDON

Connecting

Kids with

Nature

through the

Seasons

RICK VAN NOY

a natural
sense of wonder

© 2008 by Rick Van Noy
Published by the University of Georgia Press
Athens, Georgia 30602
www.ugapress.org
All rights reserved
Designed by Mindy Basinger Hill
Set in 10.5/16 Minion Pro
Printed and bound by Thomson-Shore
The paper in this book meets the guidelines for
permanence and durability of the Committee on
Production Guidelines for Book Longevity of the
Council on Library Resources.

Printed in the United States of America
12   11   10   09   08   P   5   4   3   2   1

Library of Congress Cataloging-in-Publication Data
Van Noy, Rick, 1966–
A natural sense of wonder : connecting kids with na-
ture through the seasons / Rick Van Noy.
        p.   cm.
Includes bibliographical references.
ISBN-13: 978-0-8203-3103-4 (pbk. : alk. paper)
ISBN-10: 0-8203-3103-1 (pbk. : alk. paper)
1. Children and the environment. 2. Philosophy of
nature. 3. Environmental psychology. 4. Environ-
mental education—Study and teaching (Elementary)
I. Title.
BF353.5.N37V36 2008
304.2083—dc22   2008004000

British Library Cataloging-in-Publication Data
available

Text illustrations by Aaron Alexander Hill

Acknowledgments for copyrighted material appear
on page 164, which constitutes an extension of the
copyright page.

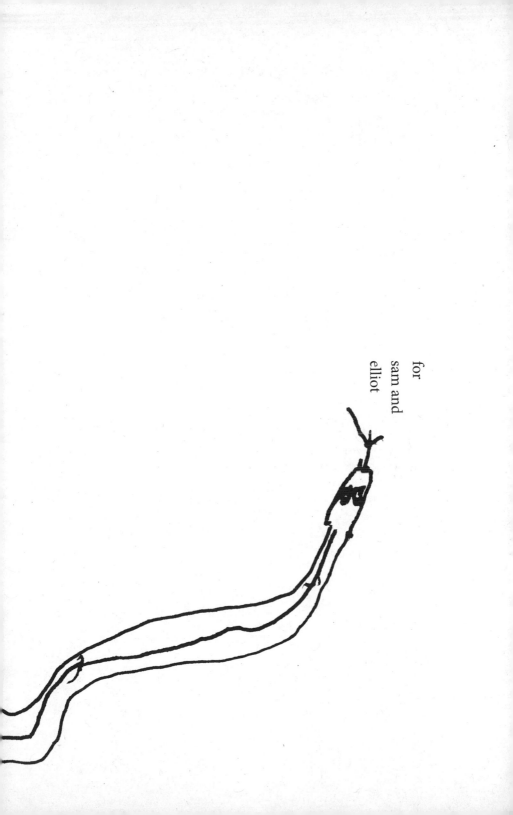

for
sam and
elliot

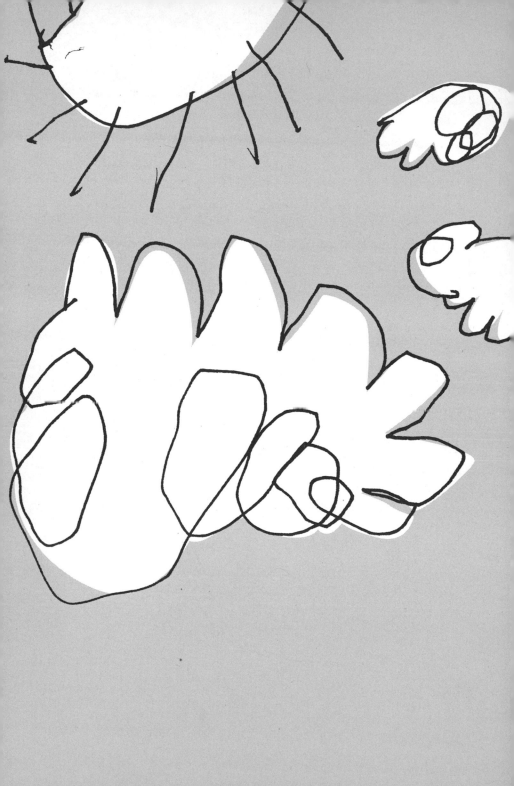

contents

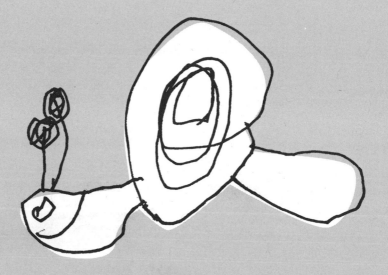

I RAN AWAY WHEN I WAS TEN. Things were fine at home, fantastic really. I had all that an American boy could want, but that day I must have grown weary with the clutter of toys and wondered where I would go if I ever did need to clear out. I hopped on the sparkly banana seat of my green Schwinn and pedaled down River Drive to where Grant Street crossed the Delaware and Raritan Canal and our little town met the highway. There was only one problem: I wasn't allowed to cross this two-lane road. Where the street intersected with Route 29 was particularly dangerous. A blind curve hid the Trenton-bound traffic. This runaway had a respect for ground rules.

Across the street and to the left stood the Union Fire Company and Rescue Squad, and next to it began Washington Crossing State Park. From where I stood on the canal bridge, heavy wooden planks soaked with creosote, I saw woods. With my friend Michael I developed plan B, no longer an escapee but explorers seeking a land route into that uncharted territory. We found two. We could walk through the tunnel that carried a creek under the highway and canal. It took us behind the Titusville Post Office and Huber's, famous for their frozen custard and broasted chicken. Farther down River Drive, near the site where General Washington and his army crossed on Christmas Eve, we could use the new footbridge built for the 1976 Bicentennial. We rode up over the Johnson Ferry House (used as a headquarters in the war, we were told) and into the 2000-acre natural area that is the park. We moved on, up Continental Lane, used by the colonial militia themselves, down past Green Grove and up the creek to the sledding hill and Open Air Theatre. Though the seats were empty, one of us usually belted out a number, something from the summer's production schedule, maybe a hatchet job on *Oliver*—weren't we street urchins too?

Then through the picnic area, whooping and hollering as the families laid out picnic blankets, tended the grill, we happy savages on a marauding raid. Onto the Nature Center, a bungalow tucked into the cedars where we brought that hawk with a broken wing with our parents and visited with our classmates. Remember Eskimo day? Venison (in place of caribou) stew and statues carved from Ivory soap (in place of tusks). Then up to the skating pond, if we had the energy, and back to the creek—a creek would always take us home, would lead us downhill toward the river, like veins lead back to the heart, but first a stop for salamanders and crayfish hidden under the red shale rocks. We saw a fox once, saw too many rabbits to count, and chased deer through twisted paths. We built forts and trails. We dammed the creek, knocked over dead trees, climbed the good ones, and threw rocks. It was the Revolutionary Army's once, but it was our battle now, until we wound up back behind the firehouse. I'll cross the highway if you go first—dare ya.

* * *

My wife and her four siblings named each dip and path of their woods. There was the Mine, site of an old coal dig, they think, and the Mounds, bumps in the forest floor and host to their bicycle motocross. They had Sassafras Grove and the Straight, a long alley of smooth packed earth perfect for gaining speed on two wheels. There was also the Back Straight, another straight off of the main one, and the Top of the Straight, a gathering place for them and the neighborhood kids. "Meet us at the Top of the Straight at four."

After school, they put on play clothes, hand-me-down plaids and patched corduroy, and headed into the woods near Youngstown, Ohio, in Liberty Township, young and free. The older boys, now architects and engineers, led the trail building, and the youngest, a towhead, was dragged by the hand or carried by an older sister. The skating pond was near the Brennans' house, and there were creeks by the Clearys' and the Overlys'. They used to climb up the ravines and slide back down. Repeat. Back by the Evanses' house survived an old orchard and a log cabin where their band of orphans lived as pioneers.

In these magical spaces, limits were tested, roles were played (or assigned), bonds were formed—with each other and with those places. Bodies grew strong, imaginations stretched, time suspended. Vigorous outdoor play, where have you gone?

* * *

Winter vacation is almost over. The excitement of the holidays winds down. Presents have been opened and visits completed. What to do now? My son, Sam, and daughter, Elliot, have watched some TV here, a little there, and have asked if they can play on the computer. These activities only seem to leave them more restless. On the last day of vacation, the second day of the New Year, I suggest they take to the woods, to a steep ravine at the end of our street and behind a neighbor's house. Joined by two friends, Alexander and Ryan, they do. These woods are impenetrable in summer, but sightlines are now open, and the kids find their way through deer paths and step on the greenbriers, ripshins they are otherwise called, for what they do to your lower leg.

A half-hour later I follow them in to check on their progress. They have reached the bottom of the ravine, thick with woody vines and tangles of branches. They crawl under and step through, hacking through the jam. At one dense, swampy area, they debate which way to go. Two want to go one way and two the other—no way to break the tie. Then the far-off sound of gunshots. This world is new and mysterious, the shots adding to their heightened senses: "Everybody down!"

By now I have been spotted, and my daughter, Elliot, tells me to leave: "Go away Dad. We want to explore. We want to make our own way." Fair enough. I have had a hard time getting them out for the past two weeks anyway, so I should be grateful for the quiet inside, and for their determination to make their own way. "Don't worry," adds older brother Sam, "we'll be home."

When they do come back, hands scraped by thorns, shins barked on logs, cheeks reddened by the roused wind, they are elated.

"We navigated through the trails and pricker bushes," offers Ryan.

"We went all the way to Staples Street," adds Alexander.

"We want to do it every day of the year," says Elliot.

"Yeah," they tell me, in unison.

After lunch, they are off again, armed with colored tape to mark their new paths. They want to build a network of trails from our

Sixth Street to their friends' house over on Third. They come back once for a pair of clippers, but are away all afternoon. I have to fetch them as the moon comes up in the east and the sun has faded behind a fan of tree limbs on the far west side of the ravine.

On the walk back home, they tell me of their plans. There will be refreshment stands at both ends, hocking lemonade and bottled water (times have changed), and they have plans for a museum for all that they've found: an animal bone, some old ceramic bowls, a metal bucket, an old bike, some Coke bottles "from the seventies" (naw, that old?), and what could be a witch's cauldron. They are sure they have spotted bear tracks, and the whole place is to be named Fox Valley, because they have seen what could be dens, and not because one of their surnames is Fox (no, really). There will be a sign, "Keep Fox Valley Beautiful," once the trash is picked up, and they will each have roles: patroller, painter, tour guide, refreshment-stand vendor, and more. Elliot's cheek has been scraped by briar or branch. Sam's knees are covered in leaf litter and bark dust. They come home full of talk, eyes wide with wonder, having gained much from Fox Valley, and they will sleep well tonight. "Thanks for suggesting it," says Elliot. This holiday season, they have received no greater gift than this.

* * *

Getting kids out into these special natural settings can be tough these days. Inside children are drawn to the flickering waves of TV and the electrifying *boing* of video games. Outside? Ripshin and other potential hazards, including fear. One of the Fox Valley gang's parents called me in the late afternoon. "I heard sirens? Are you sure they're okay?" The occupant of a house at the far end of the trail chased them off. There could be broken glass in the abandoned shed, and she didn't want to be responsible for their harm. There are roads to cross and unknowns to encounter, and they are not making unclaimed land anymore, nor leaving it alone—what was the Straight is now a paved circle of a housing development. Connecting kids to the kinds of outdoor play most parents used to know can seem downright impossible. But on the other side of that street? Wonder. Possibility. Trails to create. Animal tracks to pursue. A museum to start. A whole world fresh and new.

* * *

An *essay*, according to French etymology, is an attempt. This book is a collection of essays about our attempts to get outside. Before it was written, my kids and I began a collection of things gathered from our walks: raccoon fur, bird feathers, cicada shells, butterfly wings, stag beetles, and lots of other really cool bugs. The kids use some of these things for show-and-tell, sharing with classmates what is unique about *this* particular wisp of a snake skin.

We once found a cow molar, and one of my kids' friends said they should put it under the pillow and fool the tooth fairy, maybe double their earnings. But the purpose of such collecting is not merely to acquire, like some trip to the mall. Those objects are the tangible, friable signs of a budding relationship with the natural world, aroused by an ingrained affinity for it.

Before I built one, we vowed to put the things we gathered in something called a "science box." Pick something up, give it to Dad, "Let's put that in our science box." When its compartments overflowed, we started putting our box turtle shells and jawbones on shelves on the porch, and as we have outgrown those, we needed some other place to store these finds. So these are the *stories* of our goods, our *essays* about getting outside and of what we have brought back home.

Children aren't playing outside as much as they used to, but I leave the diagnosis for others, focusing instead on the prospects for recovery, on what can happen when kids are allowed to naturally play. I share with Rachel Carson the hope that children be given "a sense of wonder so indestructible that it would last throughout life, as an unfailing antidote against the boredom and disenchantments of later years, the sterile preoccupation with things that are artificial, the alienation from the sources of our strength."

In many of us that sense of wonder dims as we approach adulthood, but in children it becomes keener if they spend time outside—time *out*. Outdoor play can foster a sense of discovery, of exploration, and it builds relationships with both social and biological communities. It gives children all the health benefits of exercise along with the character-building benefits of play. I want to get them *out* so that, paradoxically, they develop a healthy *in*.

My kids play, on the walk to school, a game variously called "hawk," "tiger," and "horse." It's hard for an outsider, or any adult, to decode the rules. Most of it is nonverbal: they take their cues from each other's actions and their environment. One of them will unexplainably end up rolling on the ground, and the other will begin sprinting for the cover of a tree.

In his essay "Walking," Thoreau mentions a Spanish term, *Grammatica parda*, that he translates as "tawny grammar" and he says derives from the "wild and dusky knowledge of children," a kind of syntactic logic of wildness. "There are other letters for the child to learn than those which Cadmus invented." Nature may in fact know something and be willing to teach it, if we are ready students.

Each of us is the sum of our collections. This book is a collection of experiences gathered over the years of my children's lives. My children, son Sam and daughter Elliot, are now ten and eight, respectively. The essays are mostly organized by season, starting with fall and ending with summer, high tide for outdoor play. The first, "Walking to School," should contain many of the components to come: what we learn from field guides and the animals we live near, like vultures and salamanders. Many of the events in the following tales have happened after school, such as searching for a swimming hole or walking in creeks, or have been inspired by stuff we see on the walk—ordinary lawns and magical tree houses. School is all around us. Why skip class?

I'm not an expert on child development, nor do I know for certain what the right path is for kids. I'm just one father, trying to get the kids outside, and into nature.

a natural
sense of wonder

walking to school

KIDS WAKE TO THEIR OWN ENERGY. They shift from restful sleep to screaming run in seconds flat. No caffeine required. If we were surviving off the land in some faraway jungle, they might as well shout, "I am food!" As their parent, I rise too and make sure the coast is clear, and that they have nourishment to start the day.

Most mornings we walk to school, an activity that seems to take into account their natural tendency to play and explore. "Some unwonted, taught pride," writes Annie Dillard, "diverts us from our original intent, which is to explore the neighborhood."

The games start before we have stepped out the front gate. They play "hawk," which mostly involves one kid pointing out prey, the spotter, and the other diving in for the kill, the hunter. Someone is named Ruby and the other Feather. Once the deed is done, the hunter chomps and grinds its game. They sight mourning doves and mockingbirds on the electrical wires, imaginary victims. The squirrels are out too, gathering and storing food, making the same chewing motion with their jaws.

We walk six blocks to school. Our house is on Sixth Street, and the elementary school is on Twelfth. We live on a block laid out before the turn of the twentieth century when our town, now Radford, was Central Depot, midway on the railroad line between Bristol and Lynchburg. Radford is on the New River, an old river that gathers near Grandfather Mountain, North Carolina, and flows defiantly north. While the tracks follow the river, the town was laid out on a terrace above it. Once called Lovely Mount, Radford rests in a great limestone valley between the Blue Ridge and a group of narrow, elongated mountains called the Ridge and Valley Appalachians. The Great Valley it is sometimes called, extending all the way from the Hudson to the Tennessee River, transversed by the New, but long a major north-south travel and settlement corridor. When we walk, we walk southeast.

At the corner of Seventh, there's a chinquapin tree. Chinquapins are related to the American chestnut, but they have been resistant to the blight that destroyed the great chestnut stands in Appalachian forests. Spiny green burrs, "like sea urchins" says Elliot, hang from the branches in grapelike clusters. Four hundred years ago Captain John Smith noted that the Indians had a "small fruit like a Chestnut, but the fruit most like a very small acorne," so says our field guide to trees. "This they call *Checkinquamins*, which they esteem a great daintie." Some people call a cool autumn rain a chinquapin rain because the burrs fall and split open, revealing the smooth, brown, and yummy nut, a great dainty indeed. The thread of the nut that wants to gain purchase in the ground, the embryonic root at the pointy end, is called a radicle.

Beyond the tree is a ravine, mostly unexplored, home to spring peepers and probably our Appalachian salamanders before the city did some drainage work and wiped out the cattails and marsh. Something there is that does not love a wetland.

At Eighth Street, hello to Dixie, meet him at one end of the picket fence and race all the way to the other, where there is an abandoned tree house. Across the street, Megan and Brett, in a house once owned by the local florist (when Americans could walk to stores), have kept the colors alive. They have planted grapes, now purple and heavy on the vine, and zinnias, roadside confetti.

At Ninth, down the hill and behind the church, the "meadow," mostly unmowed, with five or six scattered trees with low-hanging branches and a thriving understory perimeter also untouched by the tractor. The kids have only recently ventured in there, walking through shin-high grass, peeking into a groundhog hole, into an area now known as "the woods." This kind of undeveloped land is rare anymore, especially in town. Most land suitable enough to build on seems gobbled up by commerce or convenience, but for kids, such a plot of "vacant" (as if nothing were there) ground might as well be an Eden. Certainly, it is play space, undeveloped—trees, shrubs, paths, places to hide and climb—but crucial to our human development.

To the left and in front of us is an area that used to be farmland and home to a fairground. An old picture of the area, dated 1921 and titled "Greater Radford Fair," shows tents, barns, and silos, a Ferris wheel in the background, a racetrack in the fore. They raced sulkies here, two-wheeled carts attached to a harness, the driver low behind the horse. On the day the picture was taken, people were out walking, the ladies with their parasols, once strolling where we now are.

During World War II, an arsenal moved into the area across the river to make a powder to propel bombs. When it continued into the Cold War, the housing pressure became too great to keep a fairground. Homes went up quickly, small and boxy, a local Levittown but without sidewalks. Sidewalks. How did we ever get away from those?

It's a pint-sized paradise, but there is much to see: gardens, birds, and trees, though many of them topped to avoid power lines, "hat-racked" the arborists call it, buckhorns. Whatever moniker, by preventing the limbs from growing naturally, the trees become weaker, more likely to get sick or fall, beheaded at play like Dickinson's "happy flower," apparently without much surprise.

Between Ninth and Tenth, there's a yellow road sign on a utility pole next to the alley, "Slow—Children Playing." The picture shows the boy wearing knickers and old leather shoes with a heel. Maybe the sign is left over from the time of the old fairground when boys wore knee-length socks and shorts. Now, it evokes some quaint, forgotten time before the geography of childhood changed noticeably. Its exploration has moved closer to home, often entirely indoors, so much that there may be no need for the signs. On days when there is no school, there hardly seems to be a difference on these streets. No bike riders or tree climbers, no anthill watchers or flower pickers.

We also see Joel pushing his daughter Sadie, coming home after leaving Maggie at kindergarten. Some days Joel is reading *Where the Sidewalk Ends*. Some days bald-headed Joel looks like ol' Shel. Today Sadie has a yellow and red leaf with holes in it. Hold it up to the sunlight and "it's like Christmas." I reach down to take a look and she recoils—nobody takes this from her.

Then past the Lineburgs, fellow walkers, taking their grandkids to school. "Two words," the coach says to me. "Health is wealth." That's three, but no one corrects a 300-game winner. And we do walk to school because it's healthy. And maybe it helps us focus some after the chaos to get out the door and before that of the class-room, the walk a deep breath of the day. If we had made the trip in the car, the sourness of lost library books or untied shoes might have stiffened. On the walk, the morning's conflicts fade with each step.

At Tenth Street, we hope for Pepper the one-eyed black cat, a daily appointment. He loves to be scratched so much he will drool like a dog, and sometimes follow us up the road like one too. In this crisp morning air, a conversation unfolds among the individual, the community, and the natural world. We meet the neighbors and learn the names of animals and pets, play hawk, collect things, turn them over, find out more. Learning things this way, under the open sky, seems the kind of knowledge retained far longer and more deeply than the dry stuff of worksheets. Ecological philosopher Paul Shepard calls kids' motivation to learn about animals and identify with them "loading the ark," seeing the process as necessary to the formation of the mind.

At Eleventh Street, we catch sight of spiderwebs, perfect design, strung in the dense green yews, caught nothing but the night's mist. There's more in the wet grass, spun over the whole lawn, there all along but uncovered by magic morning sun. We have seen fat white grubs in that grass, sometimes gathered up by starlings. "Look at that!" says Sam, pointing to a dying branch of one tall maple, where a northern flicker tap-taps, red chevrons on its back, gold shafts in the tail. "Here's something!" says Elliot about a translu-cent streak a snail left on the curb, another ordinary enchantment.

"That they are there," shouts the poet George Oppen, about a deer he spies in the woods, but also about anything that is something to see.

We then begin a climb back up the hill to Twelfth. Cars are lined up along the curb and out in the street, their insides fuming, waiting to empty their cargo. In 1969 half of all children walked or biked to school, according to the Centers for Disease Control. Nine of ten who lived within a mile of school walked or biked. Today, fewer than 15 percent hoof it—half of them make the trip in private cars. Fear of traffic and fear of strangers are two main reasons, but if more children walked, there'd be fewer cars on the streets. With more kids, armies of them walking home together, there could be safety in numbers—a real movement.

Crossing guard Sue greets us the same way each morning, cheerily, "Okay, come on over," offers a comment about the weather, and sometimes gives a high five to her fluorescent orange hand held up to stop traffic. Stop traffic.

Then the school itself, but woods behind it, also a kind of school, waiting to be walked through and noticed. At recess, the kids play only behind fences, on pavement, or on formal playground equipment, though they are surrounded by the fertile humus of the forest floor. When I asked the lunch table at McHarg Elementary if they would rather play in the woods, seven in ten said they would, "but we're not allowed." "Besides," added Zach, only half kidding, "you have to have a weapon, like a penknife."

Beyond the school looms the broad shoulders of Ingles Mountain, named for Mary Draper Ingles, taken from her home by Shawnees in 1755. She walked eight hundred miles from a site near Cincinnati to return home, using the New River as a guide; she and her family later ran a ferry across the river at the base of this mountain. Some days we feel like walking up the forested hillside. Last weekend we found two box turtles up there, one male and one female but on either side of the mountain, slowly making their way toward the 2,353-foot summit. At the top, there's an old fire ring with a small spruce growing out of it and rusty cans. Maybe no one camps there anymore.

From ages six to twelve, middle childhood according to experts, children naturally want to explore, expand what they know, recognize beauty, and develop affinity for creatures independent of them, as they also grow independent. The same group in the McHarg cafeteria told me they liked playing outside more than in by ten to one. Only seven-year-old Ben liked playing indoors, "because we have the Internet." "There is more room to roam," Preston told me. "Outside," said Hannah, "there are more adventures."

The hawks are migrating, the butterflies too. "Good luck," the kids have been taught to say to the southbound monarchs we glimpse on the way home. The Hawk Mountain Sanctuary in Pennsylvania reported 7,508 broadwings the other day. We should see kettles overhead soon, of hawks or the vultures that annually roost in the nearby grove of pines. Not many others are out making the journey, but most kids would like to be.

We know it is fall by the cool, foggy mornings and the tie-dyed colors, changing first at the very crown of the trees. Maybe it's not surprising we derive such pleasure from the movements of animals, the deep burgundies and bright gold of October carnival—there's a celebration out here, the town painted red. No wonder kids wake up yelling: they might also hoot and drum on trees. On some grassland or forest where the circuitry of our brains was honed, knowledge of such color and sensory detail kept us alive. We had to discern whether edible or lethal, friend or foe, how to locate a place to live and find our way back. Outside walking, we take in details of topography and weather we would miss in the car. That's why we're out here most days, standing on our own two feet, planting these radicle seeds. It's about survival.

This path might just lead somewhere.

the places i've lived, and the ones i live for

BEFORE I ACCEPTED A JOB teaching English in southwestern Virginia in 1998, we lived in a "carriage house," caretakers of a family estate in the outermost suburbs of Cleveland, Ohio. We resided in the village of Gates Mills, an official bird sanctuary, on a plain above the ravines that feed the Chagrin River. Across the street was the 389-acre Squire Vallevue Farm, a green leafy outpost nestled between the gridded streets of the suburbs and the windy trails of the metroparks, the "emerald necklace" of Cleveland. We lived there three years. At present we are sojourners in another place.

It was a great location, surrounded by fruit and fir trees, a century-old lilac bush and a good garden, a row of tea roses outside our front door. But just as we were between the cultivated suburbs and the wilder nature preserves, we were also between jobs, me finishing graduate school and my wife working a ridiculous number of hours per week in a corporate setting. Radford, Virginia, offered several benefits: a full-time job, a larger river system (the New), and the

Appalachian Mountains. It also offered the promise of affordable land. We were in no position to buy in the well-heeled suburbs past Shaker Heights.

I remember telling our Realtor several things: natural setting, old is better than new, will renovate, and, if possible, near running water and room for kids to roam.

One property backed up to the New River, but railroad tracks also ran behind the house. Another was superbly situated on a creek, a beautiful farmhouse, but we didn't go in one of the rooms because the cat population was kept in there, though the hair and smell in the rest of the house indicated that they lived elsewhere. It also needed a new roof and had a badly sagging porch. We might have been able to work with this one, but we had a six-month-old baby with us and needed a place we could readily move into.

The search has continued.

* * *

Having written a book on literary cartographers and the sense of place, I'm well aware of place writing's metaphors of putting down roots, staying put, and marriage to place. But I lived in five different states in my twenties and changed apartments or houses nearly every year. As far as places go, I've had a wandering, roaming eye. I have been unfaithful.

The love affairs started in college in Colorado, where nearly every quaint Victorian ski town looked like THE ONE but ended as merely a series of several-night stands. When I graduated my dream was to live in one of them, and some of my friends were headed for affairs with the "beautiful people," Telluride, Taos, or Tahoe—I was jealous. Before I went to Europe to travel with some friends that summer, I interviewed for a job teaching English at a school near my hometown, which would have been like "settling." At a port in one of the Greek Islands there was a sailboat looking for a teacher. The crew would be in Bora Bora by Christmas. I stood on the dock with my backpack packed and enumerated the ways I was qualified for the job, but the captain told me he also wanted a companion for his wife, and a scraggly American college grad wasn't what he had in mind. In the south of France, the mountains of Italy, I agonized over the decision, but in the end it was back to Peggy Sue.

* * *

But teaching gave me summers free, and I traveled the West in a maroon vw Rabbit with a mountain bike and skis, one of those itinerant wanderers ready for adventure at any turn. I landed a carpentry job in Telluride (skiing in that summer's Lunar Cup) but then headed to Hood River, Oregon, to wind surf, and Cannon Beach, where my friend Pat tried to teach me to wave surf. I mastered my "duck dive" under waves but was nearly slammed against the rocky coast when I tried to ride on top of them. It seemed I was looking for a playmate in places, though they wanted nothing to do with me.

In all the places I've lived, part of my courtship has involved a jog along a water feature. In New Jersey along the Delaware, in Seattle along Union Canal, in Columbus along the Olentangy, in Cleveland along the Chagrin, and in Radford along the New, running has provided a way to familiarize myself with places, to know their weather and moods, their streets and built environment, and, yes, their rivers, which in some way gave reason for the places' excuse for being. You can come to know a place by staying put, but also by running around.

In between graduate schools, after being unemployed or working odd painting and carpentry jobs in the Northwest for a long stretch, I took a full-time job in Columbus, Ohio. What place could be more plain Jane, I thought, before I moved there. Again, reluctantly, and because of dire poverty, I was dating the homely girl. But running kept the relationship, shall we say, interesting. Though the place I lived in lacked a conventionally beautiful landscape, beauty indeed comes in many forms. Yet trips to Missoula, Montana, and the North Cascades of Washington reminded me that there were other trout in the stream. Because of its socioeconomic position in Appalachia, a move to Radford, Virginia—though loaded with nearby natural beauty—could have looked like I was marrying beneath me, but we are quite happy together. Besides, I was looking for something less prissy in a place, not one of those scrubbed clean for tourists, sanitized of soul.

My family now lives in a one-hundred-year-old house in an older section of town. We have two hemlocks as old as the house straddling a taller white pine. At the edge of their drip line is a row of blueberries and beneath them a strawberry patch lined with a split-rail cedar fence. We have raspberries and blackberries too, and an apple tree and a cherry and an apricot that, though it doesn't bear fruit, blooms the first and most beautiful pale pink blossoms in spring. To paraphrase Thoreau, life's fruits are finally being plucked by us. We have two dogwoods, and the forsythia brightens yellow just as the Bradford pear's brilliant white.

Cardinals build a nest in our front hedge every spring when the wrens take up residence in the house by the shed and the cedar waxwings play in the holly. Deer have paraded down our paved street, rabbits munch our grass, and squirrels populate our tall trees. Red-backed salamanders live under the garden bricks, and an opossum once hissed on our front porch. While I was building a swing set out of native locust, a sharp-shinned hawk swiped a mourning dove out of the air. Just the other day we had a yellow-bellied sapsucker pecking into the maple.

But we are still looking.

* * *

A few years ago we came close to buying a classic yellow farmhouse that sat next to a pond and backed up to twenty acres of forest with steep hills cleaved by a drainage. For the male farmhouse seeker, this place could have been something like the equivalent of a buxom blonde or, in my wife's case . . . Johnny Depp. When we looked at the place, we spent as much time in the hills behind it as in the house. But when brother-in-law John, an architectural and fix-anything genius, flew in, he put the nix on the purchase. Where we saw a crayfish-rich creek and a swimmable, skatable pond, he also pointed out that the pond was low, possibly because of a new dam just put in by an upstream neighbor. Where we saw a sturdy, upright frame, he saw rickety construction sitting on less than a foot of field stones. No real foundation. The crawl space had no crawl. Then again, brother-in-law John is stubbornly single and lives at home.

We read the real-estate section like those living lives of quiet single desperation must read the personal ads, lured away by "Classic," "Charmer," "Nature Lover's Delight," and "Gentleman's Farm." This last ad takes us out on Piney Woods Lane to an 1860s brick farmhouse with outbuildings, but it's like an aging beauty trying not to look her age, with vinyl windows, central air, and laminate (over hardwood!) floors. The cast-iron tub has been replaced with fiberglass, the old stone hearth now a gas unit. And behind the house, a cow pasture rather than a piney woods. The land that once came with the house has been divided and subdivided. On GIS plat maps it stands squarely among a patchwork of polygons.

To make things worse, on the way there we pass the cat house, now renovated and with new copper roof—the one that got away.

"Bold stream." "The way it ought to be." "Bring the horses."

∗ ∗ ∗

I should know better, I know. Trained in American literature, I've read about the old pastoral dream of the New World Eden, the green "breast" that my Dutch ancestors behold at the end of *The Great Gatsby*, the "Big Rock Candy Mountain" (as Wallace Stegner called it) as settlers moved west. When you're looking around, you are never where you are. Lately, those flower beds haven't been weeded with quite as much care, and the berry bushes could use some pruning. But we can be analytical about these things and still not be immune to the gravitational pull of a better place.

My wife and I imagine our kids growing up in some high valley, their spirits fostered by the creases of ragged mountains, their bodies strengthened by exploring the spines of nearby ridges, and their thirst slaked by some cascading stream. This reverie calls us away to some land on Sinking Creek with a barn and twenty acres of organic hay, but it's too pricey for us. Here's one in the Catawba Valley, on a feeder stream, but it looks a little small, and is that a . . . is that a Confederate flag at the neighbor's house? We are a little like Goldilocks: this one is too big, this one is too small, still looking for the place that is just right.

Perhaps my desire is stirred by the very writers I'm drawn to:

Muir in the Sierras, Abbey in the Arches, Lopez in the Arctic, and Thoreau in the Walden woods. They've each carved out their niche in a place as I am seeking mine, but they are a monastic bunch (except for Abbey), eloquent on the need for wild places but silent on the subject of raising children. Besides, we can't all move there and enjoy it too.

There are benefits to the place where we live. It is close to schools and three blocks from the local natural foods store, but we would probably trade convenience for solitude, not that you have it when you have kids. But we tell ourselves that it's for the children that we'd like to seek out more open space. Though both my wife and I grew up in towns, she had twenty acres of woods behind her house (now developed) and enough land to keep a horse. After chores, that's where she and her six siblings disappeared. The small town I grew up in had the Delaware River as a front yard and Washington Crossing State Park in back. My little village of Titusville had some of the same benefits to living in a town that we share now. I could always find someone else to do something with, and there were plenty of kids around to kick the ball, the can, or kick up some leaves. But I don't see these games happening any more, nor do I see too many children outside in our neighborhood. Our neighbors close their windows and their blinds to keep the outside out, whereas our little bungalow, with a wraparound porch, seems designed for outdoor living.

Our "ecological footprint" is smaller if we stay where we are, since the kids can walk to school and I can ride my bike to work. Besides, kids seem just as enthusiastic about helping to plant something or make it grow, or even to clean up trash along the river or in the park—nature activities in the city or suburbs—as they do hiking mountains. This move of our culture to greener pastures is downright un-green, leading to sprawl, loss of habitat, and increased use of fossil fuels.

However, like many people I know, although we have a great place and nature all around us, we still have this desire to find a place where kids can tumble out the back door into the woods, like my wife had, or be inspired daily, like the river did me. But would what they might gain in outdoor freedom and the psychological health of open spaces make up for what they might lose in good schools and a community of friends? Why this need to own some large swatch of natural beauty anyway? Maybe we can help our kids learn to cultivate an appreciation for beauty not born of possession.

Whenever we look, they run through the meadow like colts, bound through the surrounding woods like white-tailed deer, while my wife and I kick the treads of the front steps. In the car, when discussing the property and its potential, the kids worry: I like it, but what about our house? What will happen to my room? And so modifying Thoreau's dictum—Stability! stability! stability!—when it comes to relocating with children (he would say), let your houses be one, and not three or a hundred. They need a stable place more than they need stables.

I don't know if we are staying put, or if we will pick up and go. Probably we will do both: stay where we are but use our home as a launching pad for further exploration. Where we live is not so much a result of a conscious decision, as it was for Thoreau, but we deliberately make forays into nature, getting outside as much as possible—in the garden, on the river, under the trees—sauntering on that edge between wilderness and city, desire and contentment, that Henry David also surveyed.

beautiful scavengers

THE VULTURES HAVE COME BACK. They swirl and mix above me as I ride my bike home on Sundell Drive, though not much sun reaches this shady street and there are no farmers in this dell. Only vultures. And deer. And skunks and raccoons and other animals unwelcome in town.

I declare their return when I enter the house at about four o'clock. This is the hour of lead, to use Emily Dickinson's phrase, that lazy hour after school when the kids could be outside playing, exploring, but they are watching *Arthur* and snacking in front of the tube. It has been a rough week, but this pattern of come-home-and-do-nothing is an easy rut to fall into. "Who wants to come see the vultures?" I say, as if they were an automatic draw, like Santa Claus or the circus. Today, there are no takers.

"No thanks," says my five-year-old daughter, Elliot.

"Not right now," adds her seven-year-old brother, Sam.

The temperature has climbed to 67 degrees, warmest January 13th on record, but don't look for a causal connection between the warm day and the presence of the vultures, although they seem a portent of something. That they are back is notable because the city I live in has tried so hard to chase them away. There has been a roost in Radford, Virginia, at least since the 1950s and 1960s. About 1,200 lived in the Army arsenal property on the New River about two miles away, one of the largest roosts in the East, but within the last five years some 200 of them started to move into town. Nobody knows why. Possibly, the vultures moved as a result of a timber harvest, though they lived on a steep river bank—not a good place to cut down trees. Possibly, they were chased out of the arsenal in the same ways the city has tried.

When the whistles and firecrackers local residents used failed, the city purchased a $600 propane-gas cannon to noise them out. When that proved futile, they called in the feds. Last year the USDA Division of Wildlife Services (formerly Animal Damage Control) hung four effigies in the woods where the vultures reside: THIS COULD BE YOU. They shone laser lights to flash them out and sprayed water to flush them out, but the vultures are back.

Michael Vest, the current animal control officer in Radford, has a device called a "bird banger," like a pistol for shooting blanks. It scatters them for a while, he tells me, "but they don't care. They come back." But Vest has a job to do, and when the residents make noise, so does he. "Personally, I don't mind them," says Vest. "They have a purpose. I think they're beneficial."

Several weeks later I give it another try with the kids, and we drive down to the spot where the vultures are known to roost. "I'll be the leader," Sam volunteers, and he chooses a deer path that avoids the brambles on the forest's edge. Elliot follows up the wooded hill toward an opening in the tall white pines. We see deer scat and a groundhog hole and a few vultures that appear through the openings in the branches, but none has landed and we can't get close enough to really see them. We know we are in the right spot, however, because of the frosting of white vulture poop sprayed over the pine needles, cones, and twigs. One tall pine on the edge of a clearing is coated with a silvery gray sheen—their main stand. Near the spot, four large pines have been cut down, evidence of yet another attempt to eradicate their type. Sam whacks his way through the woods, clearing a corridor with a stick, jumping over fallen trees, as much up for an adventure as he is for studying a piece of an ecosystem.

Though Vest says they have a purpose, vultures fly with jaunty indifference, not the dignified grace of a bird of prey. Raptors hunt with intent, while vultures, members of the stork family, wait for accidents. Perhaps it's their opportunism that so unnerves us about them. They glide more than fly in an unsteady path, criss-crossing over and under one another, picking up speed on the downward tilt and raising up, only to turn back into another draft. And unlike a bird of prey, they fly together, nature's version of a street gang. More likely, it's the role they play in nature's cycle: they are "tearers" of flesh (from the Latin *vultur* and *vellere*, to tear), and you can have the pun. Their cousins bring babies, but they are the undertakers. Eagles will perform this same function, would readily choose carrion over livestock, yet no one is trying to blast them out of their sycamores.

* * *

I know of two times my little town has made it into the national media, and both relate to our fowl. We made it into Annie Dillard's *Pilgrim at Tinker Creek* shortly after we tried to chase out the nonnative, noisy starlings. Then, too, they fired shotguns and cannons. "BANG, went the guns; the birds settled down to sleep. . . . YIKE OUCH HELP went the [distress] recordings; snore went the birds." And an August front page of the *New York Times* carried this headline: "Beady-eyed Stinkers Feast on Urban Fringes." The first line of the article reads, "The day the vultures arrived here was a moment made for Hitchcock." But the vultures don't really blacken the sky, nor do they attack people (nor are they the sparrows, crows, or seagulls featured in the film). And though vultures, the article goes on to say, "like being near people, with all their roadkill, livestock and landfills," people don't seem to like them near us. Last year, David Fields, the former animal control officer, told the local paper that people were worried about pets, disease, and children. I'm here to say they are good for the children.

Unlike a TV, vultures can't be turned on and off. Nature can't be controlled so easily, as my city has learned. Although nature shows on TV sometimes motivate us to get out, they create false expectations. At the pond's edge, kids want to see fish jumping, frogs croaking, and snakes slithering—instantly and right now—so nature is a letdown. Our vultures won't allow us to get close enough even to photograph them, but they provide opportunities to learn things kids won't gather from TV, like exploring their immediate world, developing their natural curiosity, and discovering what beauty might be.

The *Times* article describes vultures as "beady-eyed," but my children and I have never thought so. More likely the description comes from the cartoon image, the one with the long neck, and not an actual sighting. "Beady-eyed" also attributes a kind of malice to these creatures, an intent to do harm. What humans may see as malice from the ground are eyes finding breakfast from the sky.

The reason residents wanted to get rid of the vultures seemed to be motivated by some combination of fear and revulsion, for the work that vultures do is not pretty. But there is no evidence that they transmit disease, nor is there any that they have harmed people or pets. "They're not built to do that," says Keith Bildstein, zoologist and director of conservation sciences at Hawkmountain Sanctuary. "Their beaks aren't strong enough, nor are their claws." And their digestive system, adapted to eating putrefying flesh, breaks down microbes. Rather than spread disease, Bildstein says, they likely reduce the transmission of it, since they clean away carrion. A book we check out from the library calls them "nature's flying janitors."

Kids learn all too readily the cute and cuddly aspects of natural creatures, but they need to learn the vultury side too. In a given day on PBS, kids can watch purple dinosaurs, yellow big birds, and a menagerie of lemurs, aardvarks, bears, and fish all talking, hugging, smiling and acting nice. Are any of them hungry? Are any of them scavenging for their next meal? Some of our favorite family movies are about animals with human feelings—*Babe* and *Homeward Bound*, for example—which might be one way to learn to empathize with animals, but most of these movies minimize the disagreeable and present animal behavior in what ecological philosopher Paul Shepard calls the "sentimental cloak" of the Walt Disney view. Vultures appear in the 1967 film *The Jungle Book*, in which they have a shaggy appearance and Beatle-like accents. Though they befriend the main character, Mowgli, vultures may have been the perfect vehicle to express the anxiety felt by the culture at large about the Fab Four.

To the ancient Egyptians, vultures were deities, emblems of motherhood, giving life and then later taking it back, and to Mayans they also represented fertility. Persians accorded them royal status because of their size and the elegance with which they glide, and the Romans used them to represent military strength. For millennia the Parsis of

India have relied on vultures to dispose of their dead, but, unexplainably, vulture populations have been in decline throughout southern and eastern Asia, forcing this community to reconsider an ancient practice. Tibetans still practice "sky burial," where human corpses are offered to the vultures or Dakinis ("sky dancer"), the equivalent of angels. Tibetans are encouraged to witness the ritual and to confront death openly, recognizing the impermanence of life.

But to many Americans, buzzards, as they are frequently called, are bottom feeders, "flying rats" according to the *Times* article. Metaphorically, a vulture is a rapacious person, or anything that eats away at us. In Shakespeare's *Titus Andronicus*, Tamora appears as the figure of "Revenge: sent from the infernal kingdom / To ease the gnawing vulture of thy mind / By working wreakful vengeance on thy foes." The family name of New World vultures, *Cathartidae*, comes from the Greek *kathartes*, related to catharsis, for a cleanser or purifier, but most would clean them out rather than celebrate their cleansing properties.

Rachel Carson has said that children need to experience "the sense of wonder" before they begin to learn to identify species and name parts, that it is not half so "important to *know* as to *feel*." An emotional response, especially to the beautiful, paves the way for wanting to know, but such a response is tricky with vultures, which are not conventionally beautiful, at least up close. We admire the vultures when we look skyward on our walk to school, for they are nothing if not beautiful in flight. And we wonder at the way they cluster together, but this wonder is also increased by the knowledge we have learned. Each feature of the vulture is an adaptation, evolved to help it survive under the conditions in which it lives. The lack of feathers on their heads, for example, allows them to plunge into carcass cavities and come out clean. Without feathers to trap parasites, vultures soar disease-free. They stay at night in the cover of the white pines to prevent heat loss, and they will urinate on their legs to cool themselves down, a feature especially interesting to the younger set.

We learn to tell the black vultures apart from the turkey vultures or, for birders, TVs. Black vultures fly flatter, without the dihedral or V-shaped wings, and they will flap more. The easiest way to tell them apart is that black vultures have a black hood, but they are also a bit smaller. In the air, turkey vultures have a gray shading across the bottom of their wing; on black vultures, this gray area is out near the end of the wings near the feathers that fan out like a hand. This "telling" birds apart is learning a language. To *tell* is etymologically related to *tally*, and so telling one bird from another is to re-count the signs that indicate its meaning.

We also come to know that turkey vultures can hunt by smell. Since black vultures cannot, they play follow-the-leader to fresh kill. After a meal, they are sometimes too heavy to fly, but if a predator comes around, they will vomit as a defense mechanism. Bob Sheehy, a biology professor at Radford University and avid birder, tells me "they won't give up the calories easily. The last thing they want to do is waste a meal." Bob once raised a two-week-old vulture and describes it as "the cutest guy" who "loved to have his head scratched," but the vulture did throw up when they entered the room. "We cleaned it up like you clean up after a baby," and they named him Puke. Sam and Elliot have just gotten through the flu, and so they wonder at this defense mechanism. They also wonder at Bob's Christmas present: one year for Christmas, his wife, Kate, put a deer carcass on the roof to attract vultures for Bob to admire. Vultures are hard creatures for most of us to love, but Bob and Kate see them as a gift more than menace. We can learn to cherish the world we are given, or we can make a lot of futile noise in the forest.

And yet we also marvel at what we don't know about vultures. Why are they here, for example, in the ecotone between the neighborhood and the nearby countryside? The fact that they live nearby may make them all the more interesting. And why do they cluster together? Scientists think they roost together to share information. The pine trees are the coffeehouse or tavern, gathering places where vultures catch up on the news. And while scientists seem to know what they eat, no one knows where they go each morning when they drift over our house and head southwest. They will return at night, as if punching a time clock. "They're going off to work," we joke, when we see them from our upstairs windows as we shower, shave, and prepare to do the same.

But these are human-centered comparisons, and in nature writing vultures are practically symbols of biocentric thinking. In "The Dead Man at Grandview Point," Edward Abbey sees "V-shaped wings in the lonely sky." He thinks of "the dead man under the juniper on the edge of the world, seeing him as the vulture would see him, far below from a great distance." And he sees himself "through those cruel eyes," looks down at himself "through the eyes of the bird," soaring higher and higher, beyond the "curving margins of the great earth itself, and beyond earth that ultimate world of sun and stars whose bounds we cannot discover." In the poem "Vulture," Robinson Jeffers imagines being "part of him": "What a sublime end to one's body, what an enskyment." Jeffers imagines his body living long after his bones have been picked clean. But how do kids learn to see from the perspective of animals when we are all, as poet Mary Oliver writes in "Vultures," "Locked into / the blaze of our own bodies"—and minds?

Although the Radford vultures have a schedule, for spotting them up close, they don't often fit ours. When I see them during an early morning run, they have crossed the street from their night-time beds in the white pines eastward to the tall tulip poplars. There, they gather together in the high limbs and turn their backs to the sun, warming their wings and stretching them out to dry, waiting for the breezes to begin. They are preening their feathers and spreading their wings just as my kids are rubbing their eyes and stretching their arms. And when the birds return, at dusk, we are winding down from the day, cooking dinner and getting home-work out.

One day on my way home, I spot a woman clutching her pink sweater-wearing poodle as the vultures fly overhead.

"What do you think of those vultures?" I ask, after stopping my bike.

"I don't know what to think of them," says the woman, who will only identify herself as Mrs. B. ("I'm terribly shy.") "I don't have their minds."

"Should we get rid of them?" I ask, expecting to get a good vulture-hating quote out of the poodle owner.

"I'm an animal lover, animals of all kinds, so I think we should let them be."

We looked up at several flying overhead, their wings spread wide above us. Cormac McCarthy says they look like "bits of ash in an updraft." For Mary Oliver, they are "large lazy butterflies." When they churn in air they are called a kettle, and if there was music for their flight it would be Wagner's "Ride of the Valkyries."

I say they look beautiful. She says, "Yeah, but not up close." She had one on the porch once, clutching her chair ("the mark is still there"), and they saw each other face to face. "He had the most expressive look. Full of such expression. As if to say, well, here I am."

* * *

When we came back from our first trip to the vulture roost, Sam had forgotten the day's date with PBS Kids and stayed outside, exploring the backyard, a different kind of TV floating high above him. But we made one more attempt to get close. One night after homework and before bed, Sam and I slipped out to try to see them. By now Elliot had grown tired of vulture talk, so she stayed home. "Those crazy birds have naked heads."

I turned off the engine and lights and coasted to a parking spot. We closed the car doors quietly and heard only the crunch of our boots in the March snow. We looked up and saw a large, solitary form in a leafless tree, but the beam on our flashlight couldn't reach that high.

Sam thinks it's an owl, so I hoot. Nothing moves. Beyond the lace of pine needles and clouds drifting across the night sky, beyond the layers that obscure our vision, are stars. We tiptoe and crouch to get closer to the form, almost underneath, but I step on a stick, break it, and suddenly the trees come alive. The vultures flutter and scatter off into the night, a loud crashing of wings and branches. We duck and cover our heads and flee the woods. "That gave me the creeps," says Sam, and we head home exhilarated by our contact with vultures but sorry to have upset them. We are content to leave the vultures alone, for now, and study them from afar, as vital pieces to mysteries that soar above us. Soon they will disperse to caves and wooded mountaintops to nest. Like thoughts, it is enough to know they exist even though we cannot see them.

scorched earth

"WE ARE LEAVING IN TWENTY MINUTES," I announce, making clear our intentions to get out this winter Saturday on a hike. I must declare our time of departure early so as not to spring it on the children or surprise them, even though they know this moment is coming. Earlier in the morning I had asked if they wanted to go on a hike today, and the kids agreed but didn't want to leave anytime soon. They first wanted to play and have the morning to themselves. I try to justify why leaving early is a good idea, but my argument has no effect.

"I want to play," Sam says.

"But you can play later," I say back. "And besides, I don't want to get bogged down here all morning." Our mornings sometimes follow the pattern of one of our favorite books, *If You Give a Pig a Pancake*. In the story, if you give a pig a pancake, he'll want some syrup. Syrup will make him sticky, so he'll want a bath. Pretty soon you're writing letters and packing for a trip and wallpapering a tree house, and then the sticky paste takes you back to syrupy pancakes.

Sam doesn't like the first warning and is silent at the rest. As he hears it, or perhaps just after, he gets out paper and markers and starts in on a picture. I warn him just after he gets this project out, because he will bring to it a laserlike focus and will not be easy to interrupt. He's drawing a picture of squirrels in trees that say, "Do not kill my friends," to be used for rain forests or even local oaks—some early political art. Elliot grabs markers and paper too and starts in on her own artist's statement. Because I like the kids to play and draw, they're not making this easy.

But I am anxious to leave and have prepared the sandwiches, my wife's winter outing favorite, Underwood Deviled Ham with yellow mustard. The hike is my idea, so Catherine leaves me to do the packing. I have filled the water bottles and packed the fruit. While Sam is drawing, I start to clean the house, but where to start? I make the beds first and then start picking up the books left scattered on the floor. Would I rather have them read or be neat, I have to ask, because certainly there's creativity in this clutter. Eventually, it's on to the Legos, spilling out of their containers, and the Barbie clothes that jumped out of their baskets. Appalachian poet Jim Wayne Miller writes that children are "sorcerers" for the way they turn houses upside down, and in his "Saturday Morning" he too finds "books, bats, balls, dolls and teddy bears / with idiot smiles—the contents of every bedroom / spilled like puzzle pieces over floors."

I pick up a half-empty container of animal crackers and a juice box, and am starting to curse under my breath. It's also a winter day, a day we were going to go skiing, my favorite winter pastime, but the weather hovered around 60 degrees all week and there's no snow left. I have to readjust my time clock, programmed for winter sports. Plus, I didn't sleep well last night, a slumber-party night, when I get kicked out of bed and the kids join Mom in my place.

I am mad for the mess and mad that I've had to say something to Sam to get us out the door today. Like Miller, I want to nurture the imagination and relish in this sorcery of the ordinary, and Sam's intonation, "but we're playing," is hard to argue with, but soon the beds will be stripped of their blankets to make pirate ships, the couch cushions will form parts of alligator habitat, and all the animals, stuffed and plastic alike, will all play roles in the theater, and I might end up picking it up. I understand Miller's teddy bears to have "idiot smiles" because they have no reaction to the room. Perfect parents must smile all the time, as should their perfect little children.

I take to the outside in part to save the house from being further ransacked, and often to replenish or let off steam. Anyone who has raised young kids has at some time or another wanted to scream, and I've had my share of inappropriate responses. Nearly every time I reach in to buckle kids in a car seat and am welcomed with sticky hands or a furry, fuzzy animal to the face—then bump my head on the door frame—I've wanted to unleash a chain of expletives. It's not found in any of the parenting books, but getting mad can be a very effective tool, more simple than the carrot, not quite as harsh as the stick. And I must admit to being frustrated at how raising kids can be an incredible drain on time. Before children, I used to ride and run, heck, I used to read, and I would hike, and that's why we're going out today, goshdarnit, whether rain or shine, foul mood or perky idiot smile. Since you can't beat them, have them join you.

I leave for the local whole-foods store, Annie Kay's, to get a few "carrots" for the trip, some espresso beans for the adults and some cocoa-covered almonds for the kids. I also pick up several gold-covered chocolate coins, treasure for those who make it to the end of the trail. I will tell them about this treasure and hide it under a log when we get to the top. They're on to me, but we keep doing it anyway. When I return from the store, we're still not ready. My tension has rubbed off on my wife, and she has yelled at Sam for tracking mud from his sneakers through the kitchen. I had to put them back on while he colored. He lies on his stomach and gives me a foot, heel up. He comes out crying and sulks in his car seat. But we have finally crossed that most important stile a hiker with children must cross: just getting out the door.

We pick up Rob, our doctor, and his son, Noah, who is in Sam's first-grade class. Rob is a kind, humble man who loves to spend time with his kids and is open to alternative forms of medicine. "Americans think there is a pill for everything," he says in the car, when talking about his recent trip to China and the healing art of massage. In the middle of the conversation, the kids have gotten into a fight over a toy and Noah says, "God damn."

"Noah!" Rob yells, though he's not particularly religious. It's more that he's worried over the impression he makes.

"He picks that up from his older sister," he assures me. "Sorry about that."

The hike we are going on is named Scorched Earth Gap because, our guidebook says, a woman came to the steep part of the long hike and yelled such profanity that she "scorched the earth." I tell Rob he need not worry about the cursing, and I relate to him our own story. When Sam was three and home with his mother, he asked her permission to do something, like watch a favorite show. Sticking to our policy of limited TV, she told him no, that he'd have to find something else to do. He stayed there for a few minutes, holding back what we call a "shibba," where the lower lip sticks out in a pout. "Fuck," he blurted out.

The tiny preemie she first held in her womb, whose glass incubator she stood over in the NICU, whose regular breathing she willed out of him so we could go home, had used the language of a foul-mouthed sailor, defiling the room. With a word he rendered her speechless, until she called me.

We don't know the precise origins of Sam's use of the phrase, but it probably came from me. I am, after all, from New Jersey, where the governor joked that the middle finger is the state bird. My accent comes out, I'm told, when I'm talking to plumbers and hardware store salespeople. And, having spent some time in the trades, let's just say I've learned to express myself when angry. Probably, he heard it in the car when someone cut in front of me.

Sam uttered the word several more times before he stopped. Sometimes, he would hold back but not quite: "I almost said FUCK but I didn't say FUCK. What? I didn't say FUCK? I'm only saying it now." Each time it came out it was like glass breaking. We tried not to react too strongly lest he sense how powerful the word could be. Kids discover the power and play of language through the potty variety, but the F-word crosses the line.

In guidance class in school, the kids have learned more effective means for expressing frustration or anger. They have learned to scream into a pillow or hit it, to run around the house a few times, or to draw pictures of the thing that makes them angry. In our house, we have drawings of a parent saying, "No, no, no" with an X marked over the drawee. These papers are then sometimes crumpled or ripped to pieces, their subjects X-ed out, as we say in New Jersey.

As bad as the F-word in our house is the W-word, "whatever." I hear it much from the college students I teach, but we don't allow it. It means I don't care, I refuse to become engaged or exert effort, and I will show no passion or exuberance. My primary duty is to fit in, and since we all have our own opinions, and I am not curious about anything, whatever. Even worse is the B-word, as in "I am bored," as if the child must be constantly entertained. For use of the B-word, my wife and I might not wash the mouth out with soap, but we offer this standard advice: go outside. Get out of the house and get outside of yourself.

* * *

Catherine, Rob, and I hike through a woodland and then into a pasture and along Catawba Creek and a tributary. As the road and parking lot fade into the background, the morning's anger has dissipated too. Noah, Sam, and Elliot take off out in front. Eventually we can no longer hear their shouts and cheers as they skip on ahead. Occasionally, at a crucial junction, like the one that says "No Trespassing" (an old sign, we tell them), they wait. They hike like dogs, running forward and then doubling back to check on our progress, then bounding forward all over again.

For the first hour, the hike goes well. We find our rhythm. We see a scooped-out trunk and remember the beginning to our Richard Scarry: "My name is Nicholas and I live in a hollow tree." We point out a bird species, a kinglet, and almost hear the burble of the nearby stream over the shouts of the children. When hiking by myself, I drink in the silent woods, and I might stop and look. But kids are constantly moving, jumping, talking, although they may just stay in the creek that crosses the trail and look for salamanders, in which case we won't get very far. For John Muir, the hills and groves of the Yosemite Valley were temples, the mountains cathedrals, and everywhere in nature he saw God's grandeur. When I hike with kids, I tend to look at nature less as sacred but more as playground. I am constantly looking for a rock we might turn over, a log we might walk across, or a tree we might climb. And everywhere there could be fossils, or wild things, or caves to hide in. Before nature can become sacred, it must be accessible. It must be lain in and walked on, climbed up and run down. It must ooze between fingers and toes. It must be eaten, whole, and again.

But our energy eventually fades. Elliot is the first to go. There's a *New Yorker* cartoon that shows a set of parents in the woods with their kids. "This is hiking," they say. "It's walking you don't like." Though two years younger, she keeps up with the older boys, but when she gets close, they pick up their pace so as not to be passed. My wife, middle child of seven, relates to always having to be fourth on such outings.

A third of the way up, we are so warm that we shed some clothing, a choice we now regret near the top. After two hours of huffing and puffing up switchbacks, we are feeling tired. Elliot and Catherine have turned back. Noah, Rob, Sam, and I are pushing on. At lunch, we had asked another passing hiker how far to the top, but he didn't know, and with kids, we are better off taking things as they come anyway. It's most often when we deviate from some plan that either one of us gets mad. Another half-hour and we also turn back before the summit, an act unthinkable before I had children, but it is the right thing to do. The kids would rather play anyway. Noah and Sam are acting like dinosaurs? Cavemen? They grunt words and use hand gestures. Neither Rob nor I knows what they are saying, but the kids are clear to each other, and the message is simple: "Follow us. We know the way."

And while the kids surge ahead, neither Rob nor I, an MD and a PhD, can remember exactly the physics of why it gets colder at higher altitudes (because you are farther from the heat absorbed by the earth's surface). "Though I'm freezing," Noah says—we are all a little slaphappy now—"I remember my manners." And though we are tired, cold, and stupid, we skip along, and do not curse at all. On the way back, I slip down the steep part, the scorched earth part, falling on my tail, and everyone laughs. No one has cut me off in these woods.

When we get to the lower elevation, where the forest meets the more level pastureland, our fatigue dissolves and we feel a resurgence of energy. We meet up with the girls and read the plaque dedicated to "trailbuilder and friend" Andy Layne: "May he lighten your step. If he sensed you were tired he would say he was and would request a rest, then he'd tell a story so you'd forget how tired you were." We've been trying this diversion tactic all day, asking the kids what they might like to have for a snack later. "If I were to fall over, don't any of you SOBs put your mouth to mine and bring me back to life. Let me die right here," Layne was known to say, perhaps the closest he got to swearing.

Rob, mild-mannered Rob, from a good Jewish home, looks back over where we've come: "Holy hell," the good doctor says, "that was a long-ass hike." Our step is a little lighter, and we are unburdened of the social taboos of vulgarity, even in the presence of first-graders. Smelling the end of the trail, the kids' pace seems to slow some for a moment, as if they don't want the hike to end, but soon the games have resumed: follow the leader, daddy's the vampire, everyone hide! "In the woods," Emerson says, "is perpetual youth." For poet Jim Wayne Miller, "you must be born again / and again / and again." These are ecstatic moments, the kids lost in the woods, all of us returned to our senses.

On the way home Elliot asks, "Do those purple flowers grow up to be trees?" And Sam: "What is the second highest peak in the world?" The very purpose of this hike has been to awaken them to potential.

I see Rob a couple of weeks later at Annie Kay's—it is our night to cook at home. He tells me he was worn out after the hike but woke up refreshed, like his senses had been invigorated. "Me too," I say, "Like I had a whole new perspective on things." We talk of our next hike, to Angel's Rest. This time we will keep the jackets and hats. And we will warn the kids about not getting their feet wet too early. And though there may be words profane on the way up or down, or to get out the door, I cherish the sacredness of these outings. They return me to the father I want to be rather than the one I sometimes am.

nordic fun

ALL WEEK IT HAD BEEN NEAR 60 DEGREES with rain, downright depressing weather for skiers. But the snow report at the Whitegrass Touring Center website is positive. "Still snow on the ground," owner-optimist Chip Chase reports, "and more on the way." We leave before dawn on Saturday morning but are dubious. It continues to rain as we head north and west, but when we cross one final, ropy pass, 3,500-foot Allegheny Mountain in West Virginia, rain changes to sleet.

And when we pull into the parking lot at Whitegrass—a mecca for southern and mid-Atlantic cross-country skiers, telemarkers, and snowshoers—sleet seems to magically change to snow. The night before, Chase tells me, he made the necessary prayers and sacrifices to Ullr, Norse god of snow, and that morning he is laying out the "snow farm," mesh sheets held up by old ski poles to catch drifts.

The snow isn't deep enough yet, so we spend the day at nearby Canaan Valley, an alpine area with man-made snow. But the following morning the Whitegrass staff rolls out the trails and the "white" carpet. My wife and I enroll our children in a kids' clinic that started inside with the basics: boots, bindings, and how they fit together. The seven kids range in ages from five to eight.

Outdoor educator Charlie Waters and pro mountain bike racer Sue Haywood exchange names by passing a balled-up ski sock and grease the kids' faces with bag balm. Outside, the $40 lesson has already paid off: the kids put on their own skis and poles. Despite the chilly temperatures and gusty wind, Waters and Haywood keep the kids out for two hours playing games to learn movement and balance. Then in for hot chocolate and lunch next to the potbellied woodstove: bowls of steaming chili, grilled cheese sandwiches, and home-baked cookies, all included in the fee.

While the kids are involved with the morning play, my wife and I kick and glide out one of the marked, groomed trails but then leave the piste for a narrow band of drifted snow held by the surrounding trees. We make only about seven turns, but they are in downy snow and we might as well be flying. On my second run I catch a stick under the thin cover and fall forward, goggles first, giggling with delight. Today is not only about getting the kids to ski; it is about skiing like a kid.

I share the morning's discovery with Chase at lunch. "Freeheel skiing is about quality rather than quantity," he says. "It's not about seeing how many times you can go up and down mountain. It's about spending the day on the mountain." Chase and I discuss several more reasons for "why Nordic."

The first is access. Freeheel skiers can travel places downhillers and snowboarders cannot, and those out-of-the-way places are much prettier than a lift line. A left turn out of Whitegrass takes you to a wildlife refuge. A right turn takes you past a red barn and into an old orchard. Go straight up from the lodge, over 1,200 vertical feet, and enter the Dolly Sods Wilderness, a tundralike landscape where the only ground cover is a low mat of laurel.

Freeheel skiing also offers more interaction with one's environment, and it is better for you. Cross-country skiing is the most aerobic of sports (using large muscle groups in both the upper and lower body), and "Nords" rarely receive the kinds of injuries that boarders or skiers do.

Another advantage of cross-country skiing is the cost. For kids, Whitegrass charges $3, $12 for adults. A season pass is $25 for the younger set and $95 for adults—not much more than a single day ticket at most resorts. Whitegrass also has an "xc Gear for Life" program. With an initial investment of $175, kids can take their rental gear home and trade up each year until they reach adult sizes. "We basically subsidize kids and their skiing," says Chase. "We feel like it's our responsibility to introduce this sport to young people and people in this region."

Chase's fifteen year-old son, Morgan, is something of a phenom. At the lift-served area the day before, I saw him duck under the lift-line ropes just before closing time. I took a chair just behind Morgan. And at the top, I vowed to follow him down. I have been telemarking for twenty years (since college in Colorado in the mid-1980s), longer than Morgan has been alive, and for the most part I matched him turn for quick turn. But suddenly he disappeared over the groomed rim of the slope into the ankle-deep crud below, only to pop back on the piste by turning a "360" and landing, like an Olympic ski jumper, tele-style. I took big, wide, geezer turns down to the lodge.

Yet another reason to give the sport a try is the challenge. With a free heel and less boot and ski, Nordic skiers must rely more on balance. During the afternoon, Waters relies on metaphor to help kids find this. They make a slice of pizza with skis to stop, French fries, or the number eleven to go. "We call it anything but what it is," says Waters, including getting "sneaky" to bend their knees. She has them trot like a dog and bounce like a ball. They ski under hoops and slalom around them to add to the fun, and the day ends with a game of one-ski-on basketball. Sometimes, Chase will also put on a BB-gun biathlon. Even after the games, the kids are still up for play. Half of them work on a snow fort in one of the drifts, and the rest tumble down a wind-loaded overhang.

After the clinic, I ask Waters the same question, "Why Nordic?" She repeats some of Chase's answers, but contacts me a few days later: "Both alpine and Nordic are good for creating lasting relationships with the outdoors, getting kids' blood pumping, building coordination, using independent judgment, and interacting with weather, natural terrain and other people. While I prefer cross-country skiing and think it has many more lifelong rewards than lift-area skiing," she adds, "I'll take either one of them over Gameboy, computer games, and watching NFL football all day—all the things my son and all his friends are enamored with."

While I gather up the equipment to leave, I overhear Chase lecturing a group of snowshoers lined up and ready to go. "We get over 150 feet of lake-enhanced precipitation, more than Buffalo, New York." I'm no longer dubious but under the Whitegrass spell. The danger of cross-country skiing may be that it can become addictive. Soon you're checking the snow reports faithfully, optimistically, like Chip Chase. And then you're enrolling your kids, reluctant at first but now hooked, in the "Skis for Life" program. "They'll thank you," the clerk tells me. "They'll thank you for life."

skating pond

THE ESSAY THAT WAS SUPPOSED to go here won't. Since getting kids out during winter can be most difficult, I wanted to chronicle our attempts to find a skating pond. We were going to find the right one, learn how to test the ice, and feel our way on skates. From the car, I had marked several nearby ponds to try when winter came, and I knew of a good, still spot on the Little River. We would bundle up in the late afternoon, build a small fire at pond's edge, and bring a thermos of hot chocolate. But the weather the past two winters has been too warm for ice-skating.

We found some ice in the puddles across the street, both those with a packed layer and some with a thin white crust. On the hard black ice, the kids and I could get a running start and then slide about ten feet, arms waving for balance. In the smaller puddles the kids would shatter the white ice with the heel of winter boots and watch the muddy water drown the broken sheets—something once beautiful now ruined.

In the morning paper, the bad news keeps coming: ice caps melting, polar bears drowning, and northern trees once anchored in permafrost leaning over as if they are drunk. This December to February was the warmest on record, just a little warmer than the winter before.

We read of the scientific evidence, but there is also evidence of climate change in our history and literature. When Thoreau mapped the pond in winter, he measured sixteen inches of thick ice. A meticulous note taker, he also recorded the dates when the pond would thaw in spring. The average date for the ice to thaw, the ice-out date, between 1845 and 1854 was March 31. Some students from a group called Journey North have continued the tradition. Between 1995 and 2005 the average date on the same pond was March 13, eighteen days earlier. In 2006, the ice never came in.

Conservation botanists such as Richard Primack are comparing what is left today to what naturalists such as Thoreau wrote about. "Of the more than 20 species of orchids seen in Concord by Thoreau in the 1850s, for example, only 4 remain today." Plants now flower about three weeks earlier than they did in Thoreau's time. Trees leaf out earlier in the spring and shed leaves later in the fall. Season creep, they called it, and it's creepy all right. Baltimore orioles may have to move to Buffalo.

Around here, in plant hardiness Zone 6, we still have snow days built into the calendar, though we get very few snow-filled days, boots and mittens required, with enough accumulation and hard frost that sled runners don't scrape on the ground. On such mornings, my kids listen to the alphabetized list on the radio, then they put on snow pants and coats (the only time they seem to dress fast), grab saucers and scarves, and head for the hill behind our yard.

Adults look at snow like some inconvenience. Kids fall in it, roll in the soft powder, taste the downy flakes, and spread their limbs to draw up angels.

As a society, we have been good about preparing our kids for other kinds of dangers. We have "red alert" days in school when the kids have to duck down and crowd in the coatroom. When I was young, we hid under desks in case of a bomb or a tornado. The principal and teachers are worried about strangers coming in, the man in a dark van driving near the school, but about this heat-trapping blanket in the sky we say very little. Kids study maps and geography, but if sea levels rise as predicted, because of ice melt and heat expansion, the maps would need to be rewritten. The man in the van has been out there all along.

I grew up near where George Washington crossed the Delaware on Christmas Eve in 1776. In the statues and the painting of the event, he is always surrounded by big blocks of ice. I have brought my children there to watch them reenact the crossing. Each time it has been warm, and for the past several years the river has been too high, and dangerous, to cross. No snow, only rain and high rivers. Brown Christmas.

I can remember the river freezing and even people walking on it. I also remember the thrill of it breaking up in the spring. It boomed like thunder, loud pops from a gun. Thoreau said that "they who dwell near the river hear the ice crack at night with a startling whoop as loud as artillery, as if its icy fetters were rent from end to end." Winter awes us, humbles us, and without it, we may raise a generation who does not know the awe of ice and heavy snow, of nature capable of doing us harm, instead of we it.

I used to skate on the Delaware and Raritan Canal. My father remembers playing hockey outside, remembers practicing in New Jersey during Thanksgiving weekend. Friends tell me they skated on the duck pond at nearby Virginia Tech in the 1950s. An old history of the area records that in 1892 "young men of the area caught a train to Belspring and skated back to Radford along almost fifteen miles of the twisting" New River. The New has never frozen solid enough for skating as long as I've lived here.

In an old home movie, my sisters and I and the neighborhood kids do some version of skating, waddling slowly with ankles pointing awkwardly in. The surface is milky and scratched, air bubbles trapped and the surface groaning. We are bundled in hoods and scarves, well protected for when we fall in spread-eagled embrace. It was these excursions I had hoped to replicate.

We can still skate in some indoor places. And I've read about a new plastic, like an Astroturf for ice, called EZ-Slide. They are trying to blanket the glaciers in the Alps with Mylar, and they made a massive cold box in Dubai for indoor skiing. Technology may solve some of the problems we are facing in regard to climate change, but air conditioning to keep cool only makes the planet hotter. Ice, once broken, never smoothes over perfect again for skating. Skating ponds, never found, could be lost forever.

weed eaters

I ATE MY LAWN THIS YEAR. I also ate its roots. Probably a little dirt too. It was the first of April but no foolin'. We added dandelion and Pennsylvania bittercress to the greens that over-wintered in our glass-covered cold frame and ate them with a side of boiled yucca root. My daughter asked for more. Neither kid said yuck. Not even once. It was the ultimate economy: what would be discarded was on our dinner plate.

On one of the first warm days of spring, the grass finally green again, we dug out a row of yuccas to make room for a blackberry patch. We kicked spades into the soft spring dirt, cutting open the milky root—cool and moist, slippery like aloe, the color of coconut. Elliot peeled off her shoes to run the cool dirt between her toes. She jumped in and out of the yucca holes.

"I will have to dig to the center of the earth!" said her brother, Sam, following the root well into the clay layer. Sam dug and Elliot pulled, falling back as the bayonet stalks gave way. She pulled out ganglia with hairy nodules. Metal blade to dirt, shoe to shovel, die yucca die.

While we dug, we heard the chew, chew, hurry, hurry, hurry of the cardinals, as the visiting cedar waxwings whistled us on. We carried away three wheelbarrows of yucca root, yucca chunks, yucca meat.

Some yucca species are native to the Southeast, but our row was probably planted. Later that day we found out that the roots have been used as shampoo, anti-inflammatory medicine, and food. I peeled the woody skin off two roots and boiled them. We passed around the bowl of yucca, which tastes just like potato, and had it with our salad of dandelions, whose roots are also good to eat. Weed eating. Since that day, however, I have not been able to verify, in a reputable source, that *yucca filamentosa* roots are edible, so fooled after all, although we survived. A word of caution is in order: use care when identifying and eating wild plants.

In his 1962 book *Stalking the Wild Asparagus*, Euell Gibbons tried to redirect our perceptions of "weeds," especially the lowly dandelion, "herbal hero." While he did not mention yucca, Gibbons wrote of how we could forage for our food. "Children, especially," he wrote, "are intrigued with the idea of garnering their food from the fields and byways," exciting their "unspoiled sense of wonder" as they imagine how their forbears ate. Those forbears once knew how to scour the forests and field for chow; they once lived without that modern invention, the lawn.

* * *

April may be the cruelest month, but it's also one of the quietest. April is national lawn-care month, an obsession on which Americans spend $40 billion a year. In April the lawn-care industry would have us tuning the mower, spreading the fertilizer, applying weed control. "We don't own our lawns," Thoreau said, except he was talking about farms. They own us. "No yard!" he declared, but "unfenced Nature reaching up to your very sills."

By May, the season is in full swing. Every Thursday I can expect an orchestra: first the whine of the weed eater, prepping the grounds, twine slapping grass and sidewalk; then add the drone of the mowers, and finally, for the crescendo, the deafening buzz of the leaf blower. Every Thursday a white truck pulls up across the street with a white, covered trailer. Headphones on, someone clutches the left and right handlebars, joysticks, and backs the moon rover out of the trailer. Others grab the long weapons from the racks. They could be creatures from a sci-fi film, ready to avenge the mutant scourge—"Grass Assassins" is the name of one local company—but they are just the neighborhood lawn guys.

* * *

The California Air Resources Board says 2006 lawnmowers emitted ninety-three times more smog-forming pollutants per gallon than that same year's cars. According to the EPA, herbicide use has doubled between 1981 and 2001, and much of it ends up in the storm drains and eventually the watershed. The U.S. Fish and Wildlife Service estimates that homeowners use ten times more chemicals per acre than farmers. According to the EPA, 95 percent of the pesticides used on residential lawns are possible or probable carcinogens. Children living in homes where pesticides are used have shown increased odds of childhood leukemia, brain cancer, and soft-tissue sarcoma. What a toxic patch of ground we tend.

Annually, the average American lawn owner spends forty hours—

a full work week—spinning their blades. The reason we spend so much money and time on our lawns? Property values, for one. Drive though any high-rent district and houses will have white flags in the lawn—status markers—or trailers parked at the curb and hired hands on the fescue.

An astute observer of both cultural and geographic landscapes, F. Scott Fitzgerald gave the lawn a prominent, symbolic place in his novel *The Great Gatsby*. Narrator Nick Carraway comes from "the country of wide lawns"—made ever wider by the novel's chief symbol of a dream that kills, the car—so he takes up residence in a commuter suburb of New York. His shabby house has a view of his neighbor Gatsby's "more than forty acres of lawn and garden." His cousin, Daisy, in the more fashionable East Egg, has a lawn that "started at the beach and ran toward the front door for a quarter of a mile, jumping over sun-dials and brick walls and burning gardens." And the very last thing Gatsby does before he meets with Daisy? The very last thing after he had secured the mansion and the marble swimming pool and the magnificent cream-colored car with hat boxes and the shirts, the beautiful shirts? "I want to get the grass cut," he tells Nick, Old Sport, who sees a sharp line where his ragged lawn ends and the "well-kept expanse" where Gatsby's begins. The novel's final image is of Gatsby standing on his "blue lawn" that "he had come a long way to," picking out the green light on Daisy's dock. Americans are still drawn out of walkable cities to the grass-is-greener, sprawling suburbs in pursuit of a nice patch of lush lawn.

Another reason we spend so much time working on our lawns is because to fail to do so seems a shirking of our public duty or, worse, laziness. It is downright un-American not to fawn over our lawns. In a 2003 look at the economy of home turf, Ohio State University geographers Paul Robbins and Julie Sharp showed that many Americans associate "moral character and social responsibility with the condition of the lawn." People believe that the condition of a lawn reflects the work ethic of its owner.

* * *

In some of my earliest memories, I am running across the lawn pushing my toy jeep while my father mows. I watched the blades of grass bend underneath the small plastic frame and pretended that I too was cutting grass. Be careful what you wish for.

When I got older, I was handed over the pull cord to the green Lawn Boy, reputedly made from magnesium: the grass had to be cut on Friday afternoons to look nice for the weekend. Look nice for whom? I don't know, but our yard was not to look like the Murphys', whose father slept in on Saturdays. My dad liked the lines the wheels made in the grass, and he liked them straight, in a pattern. He liked his clippings bagged and his yard trim. My sisters and I plucked dandelions with a forked tool and placed them in a peach basket while my dad added a new instrument to the lawn symphony, an edger. He did not want grass to overlap sidewalk, so we became familiar with the sound of metal shaving concrete while we clipped grass around the lamppost with yellow shears. Some years later, we were the first home on the block to own a new contraption. It had a long pole with a rotating head that spun nylon cord. It strapped to my back, the engine behind my ear, the gas tank over my shoulder. Our brushy, weedy riverbank could now be cut regularly, like a lawn.

* * *

One difference an American sees traveling down a road in Slovenia, other than the lack of commercial signs that mar our landscape, is that Slovenians mostly let the roadside grass grow. Around houses they grow gardens, rather than lawns, and they actually use the grass for wheat or hay (one sees it drying in the wind on the hayracks or *kozolec*, a national symbol). After living in Central Europe for half a year, we came home in June to a neglected lawn.

Rather than cut it right away, we made pathways through it. Want the neighborhood kids to play in your yard? Put in a maze. Since then, although we keep our yard at a uniform but high cut, we have started to transform our lawn to a playful, edible, and riotous banquet of color.

Instead of a homogeneous green, a "green desert" some ecologists call it, in spring our lawn is a debauchery of pastels, a "fairyland" according to my daughter. We have the deep purple and brilliant white of the violets, the lavender of the myrtle and ground ivy—it with rounded teeth on its green leaves. Pull on them and you get mint. Purple dead nettle forms a whorl of leaves until the tip of the stem, but the last lobes are the darkest shade of purple, and its flowers a delicate pink. We also have yellow from barren wild strawberry (not to be eaten) and the not-too-far-behind buttercup.

Each year the garden gets bigger, and we plant more trees. This year we added another row of strawberries and more blues. What we don't eat, other animals do. The squirrels love the dogwood fruit and the bees the clover. This spring, we will plant native pawpaw—a tropical fruit like a banana or mango that is host to the zebra swallowtail—and some weeds, particularly milkweed. We will not spray to keep the bugs off. Instead, we hope they tear the plant to shreds. Milkweed leaves are host to monarch butterfly eggs, which the caterpillar uses to eat its way to fiery brilliance. If the monarchs don't eat them, we can eat the shoots like asparagus, or even the young pod. "Eaten with pot roast and gravy," Gibbons admits, it is "one of my favorite vegetables."

* * *

U.S. yards have grown so cosmetic that they are inedible. Nobody wants "messy" nuts, apples, blackberry brambles, or poke, creating problems for the songbirds and squirrels, the toads and insects. None of that bruised rottenness that feeds life.

On the walk to school my kids and I sometimes pass the lawn and garden of Joann and Norm Lineburg. Retiring after forty-seven years of high school football, coach Norm is an institution in our town and knows a thing or two about turf, so much that he's had one hundred yards of it named after him. "Our yard was a dirt pile when our kids were their age," the humble coach tells us. "I can still show you where the bases were," adds Joann. "Kids from all over came here and played pick-up games." "We were glad to have them," Norm adds. "I hardly ever needed to mow." Our yard is a dirt pile too, the pitcher's mound also an end zone. The hedge is a soccer goal, and the blueberry bushes catch their share of passes and home runs. Between punts the kids grab a snack. When the game breaks up they make mud pies.

* * *

On one walk home a few days later, we saw an older man out with his green canister sprayer.

"Gettin' the dandelions?" I ask.

"I sure hope so."

"What are you using?"

"Weed-B-Gon. I had something else but it killed everything. She was after me as much about the brown spots as about the yella."

A few houses up, another older man, WW II VET written on the spare-tire cover of his RV, is out with his white sprayer, browning the grass around his driveway and walk.

"What are you using?" I had to ask again.

"Tough Job. Does the job, and then some."

To many of their generation, settling in the developments after the war or growing up in them as my father did, a tidy green lawn is the dominant cultural aesthetic. It says, "I have arrived, I keep a neat house, I work hard." The aesthetic was in part created by the folks at Scotts, whose founder, O. M. Scott, "waged a one-man war against weeds." During the depression, the company rolled out two signature products, Turf Builder, a fertilizer, and *Lawn Care*, a magazine, the "Dr. Spock of yard care" according to historian Ted Steinberg.

I don't use chemicals, though I might like to. One pull of the trigger and the garden rows would be clear, the aphids eradicated. But imagine Whitman leaning and loafing on a spear of summer grass treated with ChemLawn.

And though I seem to have inherited some of my father's lawn aesthetic, I'm hoping my children will learn to appreciate a different palate. In making ours as edible and livable as possible, I hope they acquire a different taste. Children in South Korea do just fine with pickled radishes and sweet potatoes. In Mexico they learn to like hot peppers, and they'll eat seaweed in Japan. A bowl of borscht would not be uncommon at a Russian school lunch.

Stanford neuroscientist Robert Sapolsky says our adventure window for new food remains open while we're young. Sapolsky, who studies stress in baboons, told National Public Radio about his study of a troupe forced to move to new territory. "There's different plants and stuff to eat, and then you get this question of who's going to try the new foods." The young baboons not only ate the new foods, they taught their siblings to eat them too, but the older generation refused the novel herbage. Geezers get fixed in a pattern. They often mow their lawn the same way each time.

* * *

I don't know if we have as yet something that could be called an "edible landscape," but now that I know which roots to eat, in addition to our berries, cherries, and apples, our rhubarb, garden, and herbs, we are certainly close. We can also eat weeds: not only dandelion but lamb's-quarter (cook like spinach), chickweed (chopped in salads), and violet too (both the flowers and early leaves can be eaten, the latter apparently good in a marinara sauce).

We enjoy the freshness and flavor of our yard, but mostly it gets us outside, interacting with the natural world, having fun with yucca root. Our lawn and garden chores teach my children some of the same lessons my parents wanted to instill in me, being responsible citizens and members of the family, except the weeds go into the salad bowl and not the peach basket. By not using noxious sprays, they will learn that they have responsibilities and ethical commitments that extend beyond our lot, a care for more than just a perfect lawn.

* * *

A friend told me that his father used to keep a lawn of moss, which he did not eat. He lived in Fairfax, Virginia. The lawn was shaded by a high tree canopy. Each spring he would "weed" out some of the grass. Birds would sometimes peel it up and he would replace the divots, but mostly it was maintenance free. Clumps begot other clumps until he had a carpet of green. They put in a badminton court and played barefoot on it. Neighbors would show up with their visitors: Can we show them the moss?

During the same conversation, my friend's wife, Jenny, told me about a course she was taking on English gardens. One day she asked her professor about how they cut the "drinks" grass, that place for high tea and quartered off from where the sheep roamed.

"Because I've had sheep out here, and walking after them is not so fun."

" 'Scissors,' he told me. 'Long shears.' "

"And the other day I was cursing the weed eater, a cheap import that has lasted only two years, and I thought about how we are fighting a war in part for control of cheap gasoline, and I went in the house for a pair of shears."

She got down on her hands and knees and started cutting a small patch between her path and her garden and realized "there's all kinds of things going on down here." She nibbled some plantain, which tastes like mushroom. Her back wasn't sore from the machine. Too, she says she felt young and curious about all that was in this Lilliputian landscape, when seen up close: beautiful flowers and different scents, grass spiders and tiny insects. "I realized this is why I garden in the first place," she said.

* * *

My new neighbor may be too busy moving in to mow his grass. He mows only the front, and I bristle whenever the tractor swings wide into our grass. Whenever the Millers' gold Craftsman would make that mistake, my father would knock on their door. As for my neighbor's backyard, it is almost a foot high, scientifically more a meadow. The pokeweed is as tall as the kids.

There is probably a city code that I could call him on. A friend says I might say something in person, using the kids as my excuse. "I don't mind," I could say, "but I'm worried the kids might step on a snake or something." But I am not worried. Besides, young poke-weed shoots "so closely resemble asparagus some may be fooled," according to Gibbons. The kids also make their own concoctions with the pokeweed berries (not to be eaten) that stain their hands purple. Left alone, a lawn would eventually revert to a deciduous forest, a "climax community" in terms of ecological succession, and we've always wanted a house in the woods.

Daylilies grow along the alley my neighbor and I share. Their buds can be added to soups, like okra; their blossoms, tubers, and stalks can also be eaten. If the kids don't kick them like soccer balls, puffballs grow on the hill behind our house, a tasty edible mushroom (be especially careful with mushrooms).

I have heard of the Edible Schoolyard, a project in Berkeley led by Alice Waters that provides urban public school students with a one-acre organic garden, but the growing season in southwest Virginia does not coincide with the school calendar. Still, by eating both what we plant and what grows anyway, I hope my kids are getting an edible education. When they stand on our lawn, I hope they too are sensing something "commensurate" to their "capacity to wonder," a green light symbolic of a vibrant, colorful future right in front of them.

Meanwhile, the yuccas have already sprouted in spots where we dug them out. That's the nature of a weed: it comes back. Yucca flowers are said to taste like endive.

creek walking

WE CALL THEM STREAMS, rivulets, branches, and brooks. In spring they can be freshets. They are tributaries until you get to either end. This one is a run. Connelly's Run. Named for surveyor Connelly who laid out the Wilderness Road in advance of Daniel Boone. But when you are talking about playing in a "small body of running water," only creek will do. And when you hop across stones or hunt crayfish in a creek, you call that creek walking.

After school one breezy spring day, I ask my seven-year-old son, Sam, what he wants to do. Fly a kite? Ride a bike? Still thinking about the kite. Go to the creek?

"Yeah. With nets!"

We pick up his younger sister, who stayed at a friend's house after morning kindergarten. Everyone in the neighborhood is putting on roller skates or jumping on scooters. "Looks like fun," I say, worried that my children don't enjoy typical after-school activities. "Want to try?" But both their minds have already been made up.

They'd rather test their balance on mossy, wet rocks than on wheels. Since they have been old enough to walk, they have enjoyed creek walking.

It's not officially sanctioned as an after-school sport, though it requires some of the same skills and teaches some of the same values. Equally important in this digital device–crazy age, it gets kids outside, relating to their environment and with living things.

First, you need agility and balance. You must be graceful as a heron to walk over slippery rocks. And while a parent or coach can point out that a particular mossy rock is slippery, kids learn best by figuring that out on their own. If they fall, they learn to pay attention to those conditions that made the fall happen.

Creek walking also requires technique, and there are basically two kinds of creek walkers, the wet and the dry. Dry creek walkers try to cross without dipping a toe. They treat creek walking like horizontal rock climbing: plan the route, look for the good hold. Wet creek walkers are less interested in what lies on top of the rock, a secure surface, than what lies underneath, moving animals, and they could care less about keeping dry.

It always begins so innocently for us. We are there to see the spring wildflowers, the bloodroot, spring beauty, and the little Dutchman's breeches. Soon the kids are tossing stones in the creek. But then there's a particular rock to get, and a salamander under that one, and so a toe must get wet to catch it. Soon the whole leg is in. Eventually, Maclean wrote, all things merge into one, and a creek runs through your shoes.

If you would catch critters, you have to know which rocks to turn over, how not to disturb the upstream sediment and cloud your hole, and where the crayfish are likely to gather. My kids have tried several techniques: the patient one is to stick the net behind the crayfish and move something in front of it. Crayfish swim backward and usually into your net. But the kids have also mastered the art of the quick splash and scoop. Experienced creek walkers can slowly move a bare hand behind a crawdad and then lunge for the spot behind the pinchers, pinching without getting pinched.

You don't need much in the way of equipment for creek walking. Old sneakers keep out some of the pebbles and help protect your toes. A triangular net will lay flat in the creek bed, and its corners can scoop out spindly crawdads.

Finally, creek walking requires teamwork and good sportsmanship. You must learn, for example, that your little sister also wants to hold that salamander (and that you shouldn't yell at her when it slithers away), and that you should not cloud someone else's hole by walking upstream and releasing the silt. You must learn too that when the game is over, it is time to go home, even if you haven't caught that last minnow. Screaming and stamping your feet is not a gracious way to end the game.

But there's a problem with taking up creek walking as a recreational sport. There simply aren't enough playing fields.

On one of our many trips up Interstate 81 to visit grandparents, we once pulled off in a little town near Carlisle, where the highway meets the Pennsylvania Turnpike. We wanted to let the kids out to play, and we found a park with a log structure, part fortress, part wooden castle. But nearby was a clean-flowing stream, and the kids opted to play in it. The results of such an experiment could probably be repeated across the nation—kids would readily choose a good creek over expensive playground equipment—but too often we spend money elsewhere than on water quality. According to the most recent state water quality report, some 9,000 miles of rivers and streams and 2,200 miles of estuary in Virginia are "impaired." Almost half of all Virginia waterways are not fit to play or swim in.

Down at the creek, most people walk right by, Mountain Dew in hand. A few even seem to frown disapprovingly—probably never did it when they were young. Creek walking is not a spectator sport. Only participants enjoy it.

On another adventure the kids found a milk container sliced in half. At the bottom was a loop of duct tape, sticky side up, dotted with pennies to be used as ballast. And at the back of the ship were taped two cardboard tubes, probably flag posts. The kids thought they had found treasure. Soon, everything they found on their trip became part of the sea wreck. Two small pieces of frayed, algae-covered plywood must be from the decking, and a galvanized fence-post could be its bowsprit. Creek walking develops qualities that organized sports may not: imagination, discovery, spontaneous play.

The essence of creek walking is movement. Though creeks may flow over rocks that are sedentary, your kids will not be when they are near. One day I enticed my daughter and her friend to go to the creek by suggesting that we take Barbie for a swim. She shot the rapids several times. Much screaming, but brother Sam was ready with the net to rescue her from the maelstrom. Meanwhile, they built dams. Sam said he wasn't so much interested in "holding back the water" as in "making interesting flows," waterfalls, ripples, air bubble eddies. The kids used rocks to create the structure and leaves to patch the cracks, but water found the weakness, and Barbie, having been laid in the water to rest against the rocks, dove through. After several more rapids and a vigorous chase to rescue her, the girls placed her on a rock to dry and to be "kissed by a prince," an event unlikely to happen unless Prince Charming could be disguised as a frog. Or a salamander.

On yet another adventure, we kept score. On a football field–length stretch, from bridge to bridge, we netted twenty-two crayfish, seventeen minnows (of those, at least three different species), and four salamanders. Our ratio of crayfish to minnows was high only because we had so recently taken such an interest—and proficiency—in catching them. But we let everything go. We once tried to put some newts in a tank, but later we found one dry and lifeless among the dust behind the bookcase. Creek walking can teach fair play. Nobody needs to win or lose, least of all the critters.

We worked our way up to the deep pool near the bridge. Elliot spotted a large crawdad. "It's not a crayfish, Daddy, it's a lobster!" We knew there was a big one in this pool. Years ago we spotted a blue beauty with one claw, "Big Daddy." When the cousins visited from Baltimore, we took them down to our clean creek with the hopes of seeing B.D. Just before we were ready to pack it in and trudge the impatient toddlers home, my wife snatched him from the channel, gently holding him by the thorax and behind his closing claw. The kids were momentarily as startled as he was, until they hoorayed and squealed with delight. They have learned to revere Big Daddy and this spot, so full of magic and wonder.

Radford City High School biology teacher Frank Taylor has helped us take our creek walking to a new level. On a muggy Fourth of July day, we left the celebration in the park and took to the creek with long-handled nets, egg cartons, and a brownie pan. The kids scooped a netful of pebbles out of the riffles and scattered them in the cookware, sifting through them as if panning for gold. Eventually, tiny invertebrate insects and crustaceans came into focus. Through the Save Our Stream program, we learned what species are indicators of good water quality. We saw mayflies, whose aerodynamic shape helps push down on the rock surface like a racecar. If we had a magnifying glass, we could have spotted the hairs they use to catch food in their comblike mouths. We saw the caterpillar-like caddis fly and the yellow stonefly, the latter doing something like push-ups to bring oxygen into its gills. The kids learned that these species depend on clean, oxygenated water to survive, and that there is a world underneath rocks: casings of hatched larvae and tracks from the gilled snail. From creek walking, they learn.

About how this creek will blend with that river. And that river into the next. And how pollution can end up in the creek, and that if there's too much of it, these species will disappear. Along the banks, they have seen cups, bottles, and bags, which are visible signs for the heavy metals, *E. coli*, and fertilizer they cannot—the results of some bad teamwork.

One day they will walk upstream, all the way to the creek's source. They will imagine the journey that a small canoe will take, like the one in the film by Canadian canoeing legend Bill Mason, *Paddle to the Sea* (1966). It will travel west toward the New, then north where it will join the Gauley to become the Kanawha. And then west along the Ohio and down the great Mississippi past New Orleans and into the Gulf of Mexico.

Each time we return to the creek, something has changed. The seasons change, the banks change, even the well-placed rocks of the dams move or are moved by someone or something. Unlike other sports, the playing surface shifts—unstructured and loose, free-flowing and without bounds. In the morning we sometimes see a heron, and in the sunny afternoon the water reflects the colors of the trees and sky.

Each time we go to the creek, we are changed too. As much as the kids catch in the creek, they are also caught by it. Several years from now they may travel to places far away from this watershed, but for now all they need are two feet and a creek. They catch *life* in this creek. They are creek walkers. They walk in their neighborhood creek.

holy land

WHEN SAM WAS LEARNING TO WALK, we ventured out in expanding concentric circles. Eventually we journeyed beyond our backyard, across the gravel alley, through a hemlock break, and into our neighbor's yard. It had something bright and colorful that our yard did not yet possess, a swing set. But next to the swing set was an even better find, a green plastic sandbox in the shape of a turtle. Sam squatted down to look inside, and I helped him remove the bricks holding the lid down. Water drained from algae-stained pools. The inside hadn't seen daylight in a long time.

Sam had already developed a fascination with dinosaurs. I don't quite know what the lure of them is for kids, but nearly all little ones I've known have had some kind of fix on the reptilian giants. Whenever the science museum has a dinosaur exhibit, it's always well attended, and we've made the trip to the American Museum of Natural History in New York where Holden Caulfield sought innocence preserved in glass. In the main entrance, the Theodore

Roosevelt Rotunda, a fifty-foot-tall skeleton of a barosaurus rears on its hind legs, throwing out its massive tail to protect baby from a marauding allosaurus. Other kids are always there, wondering at the drama played out long ago.

For kids, dinosaurs are superheroes, part fearsome and with dangerous fangs, like *T. rex*, but part invincible, layered with a protective shell, like stegosaurus. Kids identify with *T. rex*'s ability to make an impact, to tear through the jungle with screeching roar, terrifying all in its path, or with triceratops's ability to fend off predators with bony plates. Put them together, and you have a young person's idealized self-portrait.

Sam went overboard. By preschool he could name all the dinosaurs, and when the teachers called them the generic term, *dinosaur*, he wanted to know the specific type, and whether meat eater or no.

The fascination with dinosaurs came in part from a *National Geographic* we showed him. The issue surveyed recent fossil evidence, including dinosaur droppings. At this time, he couldn't quite say "dinosaur," nor could he say "fossil," so he blended them together into one word, "diya-fossy." When he sighted the fossilized excrement on glossy pages, he saw "diya-fossy poop."

And then, beyond the backyard, digging through the neighbor's sandbox, under the leaves and debris and caked sand, lurked a red triceratops. He was a paleontologist unearthing fossies, and right here near home. The ground he walked on was now sacred, rich with the wonders of the ages, albeit in hardened plastic rather than petrified bone.

Trip after trip, we took so many diya-fossies back to our house that I finally had to knock on the neighbor's door and explain, in case they noticed that someone had been rummaging through their turtle of a sandbox. Robin told me that her little boy had outgrown dinosaurs, and we could help ourselves. We did, until all the dinosaurs had been unearthed, or unsanded.

Then one day, while digging around for more fossies, one of them moved. The search had expanded to the mossy garden bricks beneath the apple tree. Underneath one of them, something glossy and wet disappeared. Things scattered beneath nearly all of the bricks, one of them ultimately squirming and wriggling in Sam's hand. When he learned what they were, salamanders, living fossils, related to his beloved dinosaurs and coexisting with them 165 million years ago, a love affair with all things *herpeton* (Greek for "crawling things") began.

He has gone steady with snakes, dated the other reptiles—the alligators, crocodiles, and caymans—fallen for lizards, geckos, iguanas, and chameleons, and flirted with exotics—the Komodo dragons and anoles—but mostly he has remained faithful to his first love, to the salamanders.

There have been others. Our friend Justin once called us to come out to his 130-acre hollow near Ironto. "There's a copperhead in the woodpile." We drove there as fast as we could, but when Justin pulled back the tarp, no snake. Justin grew up on Staten Island when it was woods and is a New Yorker's kind of nature lover: intense and tenacious. He started pulling up black tarps near the orchard, and more than one black snake hurried off. We also found a frog in a puddle. Not a bad day for your average herp hunter, but we were still on the chase. Then, on the way back to the cabin, on a splitting log outside the door, perched a bright-orange and aqua-blue skink. We had a net, and for a brief moment we held the fella in it, but he was bigger than we were used to, faster too, and disappeared under

Justin's front steps. We spent much of the afternoon trying to flush him out, but he wouldn't show his pointy nose and long tail again.

Sometimes our encounters with reptiles have brought trouble. The ponds near where we lived in Slovenia were full of turtles, and we liked to go catch them. On Easter Sunday, we strolled Three Ponds Park with a net. Sam pulled out a red-eared slider or dime-store turtle, a feral species bought in pet stores but released. He went to pick it up and reached across the front of its shell. The turtle poked its head out and grabbed hold of Sam's finger. He screamed and shook his hand violently, but it wouldn't let go. I whacked the shell with my knuckle and the turtle dropped on the ground, taking with it a slab of skin. All the way back to our apartment Sam screamed, with half the town of Maribor strolling through the park and looking unsympathetically at us: "You don't see other kids sticking their hands in there, do you?"

The nice thing about salamanders is that they don't bite, or if they do (and some will), it doesn't hurt as much as a turtle. They're not as quick as a skink either. But the best part about salamanders is how many of them there are. We live in the Southern Appalachian Highlands, a region with a greater diversity of salamanders than anywhere on earth. "Assume you are willing to learn something about salamanders," Maurice Brooks writes in his classic, *The Appalachians*. "The Appalachian Mountain system," he continues, "is the place to do it, the best one there is."

When the glaciers receded in this area, and the East Coast began to heat up, the salamanders were trapped up in the mountains. Because they breathe through their permeable skin, these lungless salamanders, plethodons, need moisture, and the damp climates of higher elevations, which stay cool even in summer, provide an ideal habitat. Some parts of the Southern Appalachian Highlands collect as much precipitation as the rain-soaked Northwest. When properly cared for, these mountains also provide a healthy forest with an abundance of invertebrates and microorganisms on the floor, two other factors important for salamander health.

For several years now we have attended the Mount Rogers Naturalist Rally to look under rocks. There, a whole world of crawling, wriggling things is startled by sunlight, as we are surprised by their presence. Because the area is so rich for finding salamanders, such a hotspot for diversity, herpetologists know it as holy land.

There are twenty species in the Mount Rogers National Recreation Area, and eighteen of them, except the common newt and the foot-long hellbender, are lungless. When you step in some nearby mountain streams near there, the rocks seem to move, but it's only the stream-dwelling hellbender, the largest American salamander, revered enough to come by several nicknames: water dog, mud cat, Allegheny alligator, snot-otter, or just plain grampus. The Smokies brag about being "the salamander capital of the world," but the Mount Rogers area contains about a tenth of the acreage. Mount Rogers, the highest mountain in Virginia, sits in the lower southwest where Virginia meets North Carolina and Tennessee. The area also contains overlaps between extreme ranges of southern and northern species.

The first night always begins with dinner at the Konnarack community center: baked chicken, boiled potatoes, green beans, cooked apples, a biscuit, and choice of sweet tea or lemonade. In the morning, choose a field trip: trees, aquatic insects, wildflowers, birds of the crest zone, invasive weeds, geology, and more. We always go on the salamander walk.

At long tables with folding metal chairs, I sit with the leader of our first salamander trip, Dr. James Organ. Organ has studied salamanders since 1953. He spent so much time in the field near here, over the course of a fifty-year career at City University of New York, that he "got to like the people and place" and retired where he had completed so much of his research.

He focused on three main areas: distribution, demography (the structure of their population), and courtship behavior. His dissertation advisor told him he could not publish his drawings. "You drew the spermataphore to look like a phallus." So Organ took photographs of his species and presented those to his committee. "Okay. You can publish it." When he started, there was "nothing in English on salamanders." There was work by a Russian scientist who had thirty-five field technicians. "I had Della," he said, pointing to his wife sitting next to him.

Organ was responsible for establishing a salamander management area so that loggers would have to determine the damage before cutting. He also focused on how commercial collecting for salamanders, to be used as fish bait, was hurting the species. "They would scour the creek bed and throw the rocks up on the bank." Salamanders can use the same shelters for twenty to thirty years, so removing rocks or logs greatly disturbs them. To prove that populations were being affected, Organ compared areas where harvesters collected salamanders with remote areas they would not disturb. The density was much greater in the hard-to-reach creeks.

In the Southern Appalachian Highlands, salamanders have more biomass than birds and mammals combined. During rainy summer nights, the forest floor is said to move. Salamanders are the top predators of the detritus chain, getting 80 percent of their food from the soil (the other 20 percent from flying insects). When you take them out, there are more bugs. And when there are more bugs, there are less bacteria and nutrients. When there are less of those, there are fewer trees. Organ found the ultimate means to persuade the U.S. Forest Service: remove the salamanders and forest productivity goes down. "I showed that salamanders were important as more than just fish bait." He convinced the Forest Service to cut down some trees to help make nesting sites for salamanders, even with some of their prized oaks. Some weeks later he heard someone from across the aisle at the local store: "Do I understand it to be that the forest service is cutting down trees to make houses . . . for salamanders?"

Organ has also retired now from leading salamander hikes, so in the morning we meet up with Kevin Hamed, a professor of biology at Virginia Highlands Community College, and his friend Matt Chatfield, come all the way from Ann Arbor to do his doctoral fieldwork on salamander genetics.

Before we head up the Lewis Fork Trail, Kevin lays out a few rules: we must put rocks and logs back where we found them, and gently. "It shouldn't look like turkeys have fed here." And we must put our collections in bags that will have to be destroyed or cleansed with bleach when we are through. We must guard against spreading the chytrid fungus, sweeping through Central America now and killing three-fourths of the species it touches.

Every year the process is pleasantly familiar. We start up the trail a ways and then scatter and spread out, some for the seep behind the rhododendron, some for the downed logs on the hillside. "Here's one," somebody says. "I got three," cries another. I turn over a rotten log, exposing webs of rootlets, fungus fronds. Flakes of bark peel away and drop into the dark, musty soil. A world of inhabitants is startled by the scorching light, frozen momentarily before fleeing the dry air. If one is out browsing for food, it will hold fast but then scatter through an escape tunnel. Hold a little guy, and it is clammy but fleshy and alive. Little legs and a long slender body fidgets in your palm, tail twisting. After about fifteen minutes more of crawling around the leaf litter, raking our fingers through the damp, sweet humus, we gather together while Kevin and Matt hold up the bags and plastic containers and help us identify our catch.

Sam comes back with four different species. We learn of the *Plethodon montanus*, northern gray-cheeked salamander, formerly thought to be an imitator of the Jordan's salamander before they were given separate species status. We learn too that the field guide we have been using, the *National Audubon Society Field Guide to North American Reptiles and Amphibians*, the one Justin gave us after we discovered the skink, is incomplete and sometimes wrong, which is one reason Kevin keeps calling out Latin names. Even the definitive *Salamanders of the United States and Canada*, by James Petranka, published in 1998, has a hard time keeping up with new developments. Researchers keep finding distinct characteristics and regional differences, and new species are identified all the time.

The diversity of these lungless salamanders is a result of the "island" effect, "neatly showing how isolation is a force for the evolution of new species," according to naturalist Scott Weidensaul. The ridges and peaks of the Appalachian mountains are separated by deep valleys, and these "islands in the sky" are further fragmented by our modern lifestyles. Slow-moving salamanders don't cross road barriers well, so they adapt and slowly change in place.

We learn to tell the red-backed, same as under our garden bricks, from the Blue Ridge dusky (easily confused with the Allegheny

Mountain dusky). Though also a plethodon or lungless salamander, *Desmognathus orestes* is found in aquatic environments and has a keel-like tail, knife-edged, almost a fin for swimming. Even in one sample area it can have incredible color variation, a light stripe of yellow, gray, or chestnut, even variable patterning and stripes. It helps to know that this, like other members of the *Desmognathus* genus, has hind legs much larger than the front, like its dinosaur counterparts, and useful for jumping like its frog friends. It also has a line extending backward from its eye to the jaw. Sam finds a pygmy salamander as well, at the northern end of its range, the smallest of the Appalachian salamanders and distinguished by a row of chevrons on its back.

At our second stop, near a creek, our group finds one species a few yards out from the water, the stout and salmon-colored spring salamander, *Gyrinophilus porphyriticus*, if you want a mouthful. In the creek, we find totally different kinds. Elliot and I nab a black-bellied and a Blue Ridge two-lined, almost translucent. Hold it up and you can see the living heart. Look closely, and you see it beating.

Everyone gets into the act now. "If I was a salamander, this is where I'd be," says Kevin. We are all kids flipping over rocks, rolling over logs. "Here's another one." "Found one." "Here's a cute little guy." With us are Suzanne and Dan Stryk, she a painter and he a poet. Both are teachers. They are enjoying the kids as much as the salamander hunting, noting that as rare as some salamanders are kids who find joy in crawly live things. "The best scientists are the ones who never quite grew up," Dr. Organ told me. "They retain a kind of wonder about them."

Nearly one-third of the salamanders we find are missing a tail. Salamanders will shed it to escape predators and then grow it back, offering scientists some intriguing work for how this might apply in the human world. At our third and highest spot, we mostly look for species that have eluded us. Theoretically, we could begin at Damascus, "the friendliest town on the Appalachian Trail," elevation 2,000, and work our way up to the top of Rogers, at 5,729 feet, and find a different cluster of species at each interval. At our third spot, we were hoping to find the Yonahlossee (yah-nah-LO-see), the largest of the eastern lungless salamanders and the first to be identified by Emmett R. Dunn, "patron saint to the entire family of Plethodontidae." Dunn named it for the Grandfather Mountain road he was traveling on at night.

Yonahlossee eludes us today, but no one seems disappointed, least of all our five-year-old friend Max. "This is the greatest time in my life." He stops learning Latin and simply calls those he has in his plastic container Tim, Tim I, and Tim II. I ask him about the third, and he tells me it's a "sleepy salamander," yet a new species, but it awakes and crawls up his sleeve. Sam is no less effusive about letting scientific nomenclature dim the enthusiasm. "Awesome. I got an *orestes*."

Something about salamanders captures the imagination, especially among those not far removed from crawling. They are creatures of the in-between, living on both land and water. Much of it is probably sensory, as they are wet and wriggling to the touch, the forest floor sweet and musty. Perhaps it is simply because they live in damp, cold places we would choose not to, exactly the opposite of where salamanders were thought to come from. In Greek, *salamander* means "fire lizard." When logs were thrown on the fire, the salamanders would be seen crawling away, so they were believed to have emerged from fire, earning a mythical, dragonlike status. In *A*

Blithedale Romance, Hawthorne writes that Westervelt was "not a whit more warmed by Zenobia's passion, than a salamander by its native furnace," reflecting the common folk belief that salamanders were so cold they could survive a fiery blaze.

Perhaps what is most mysterious about them is that they are there, in the forest, but hidden from view. E. O. Wilson has coined the term *biophilia* for the affinity humans seem to have with other creatures, the connections we subconsciously seek with them. If we do possess an affinity for other beings, then holding them in your hand completes the circuit.

In *The Future of Life,* Wilson says there are two kinds of naturalists, those intent on finding the big animals, especially the birds and mammals (and perhaps dinosaurs), and those like himself who seek out the little things. "Let me enter a tract of rich forest and I seldom walk more than a few hundred feet. I halt before the first promising rotten log I encounter. . . . Always there is instant gratification from the little world hidden beneath." There, in the dirt and rot, the insect frass beneath our feet, are "giants of the microcosm."

But Wilson is worried about the future of life. Some species, especially the amphibians, are disappearing at three times the rate before humans arrived on the scene. The golden toad of Costa Rica is presumed to be extinct. Frog populations have declined, and deformities are turning up across North America. Atmospheric pollution plays a role in amphibian decline, as does an increase in ultraviolet radiation brought on by a thinning ozone, in effect singeing porous amphibian skin. Nonnative fish such as brown trout feed on native frog species. Habitat loss, especially of wetlands, plays a major role, but in Central America the chytrid fungus appears to be the main culprit, a kind of smallpox of frogs. Amphibians are the canary in the coal mine, sensitive to atmospheric conditions, a bellwether of environmental health. They survived the K-T (Cretaceous-Tertiary) extinction that wiped out dinosaurs, but they may not fare so well in the era of human disturbance.

On the way out of the woods, little Max says wistfully, "I'm gonna miss this place." So far, frogs and salamanders of the Southeast have held up well, so we can all come back. But perhaps the future of life depends on these kids, and on their knowing how important this place is for salamander health. From our backyard to the mountaintop islands, from the dense hardwood forests to the spring-fed waters, this land is a holy land, made for you and me and all things that crawl.

bridge 33

IT HAS BEEN A GREAT SUMMER FOR FISHING. With a blood worm and a split shot, seven-year-old Sam showed up the guys and their surf rigs on the Virginia Beach pier and caught the largest flounder of the day, its sixteen inches only half an inch under the limit. And he beat all other fishermen one day at the lake in the Poconos, including his grandfather, by landing a sixteen-inch pickerel, the only non-panfish brought to shore. He also caught the largest bass his cousins had seen in the pond across the street from his uncle's house in Syracuse. Though it barely fit in our white joint-compound bucket, we brought it up to the house to show everyone, giving it a temporary home in the galvanized tub that held last night's round of beers.

We don't quite know where he got the idea, but while gazing at his proud catch, made more venerable by the admiration of cousins and aunts, he decided he wanted to stuff his bass. On family vacation, parents especially want to make their kids' dreams come true, and for a brief while, we actually entertained the idea: how could we keep it cold until we got home, or find a taxidermist while traveling? In the end, after a struggle much harder than landing a big fish, some form of reason won out, and we convinced him that this fish wasn't a true treasure because it didn't come from his wilder home waters.

I think he must have first seen trophy fish mounted on the wall at the Buller Fish Hatchery near Thomas Bridge. We stopped at the office after a disappointing day last year on the South Fork of the Holston. If we couldn't catch a fish, at least we could look at some up close, even those dusty and lifeless on the wood-paneled wall.

I fished there the previous day and caught several wild rainbows, but I also saw two snakes and a toad. Then, my son was as much interested in reptiles as he was fish, so I convinced him to go, in part, to catch creatures of land.

The South Fork is a good place for us to go. There's a stocked section just above the dam where the fish hatchery intakes its water. From a platform deck, so the plan was, he could fish for trout with a spinner or worm while I worked the tailwater or the upstream special-regulation section with a dry fly. He had little action, probably because that area receives so much pressure from the trout stalkers, those who follow stocking trucks, while I landed a rainbow just below the dam. I tried to bring it over so Sam could play the rod and reel the fish in, but while watching Sam crawl down the bank I slipped, and the fish got off before Sam could behold it.

Our first duo fly-fishing experience actually happened two years ago in Slovenia. We stayed at a bed and breakfast in the Logarska Dolina (beautiful valley) with some friends. Chris and I rose early to fish the nearby stream. We put on our waders outside by the porch to the tune of cowbells and a polka coming from the milking barn. Then we walked through the field of spring wildflowers and down to the stream, a "Hills Are Alive" moment if ever there was one. I caught a beautiful brown in the riffles behind a rock and worked my way up to the bridge—where Sam was waiting for me. He woke up, saw that I was gone, dressed his five-year-old self, and ran down to the stream. I tried cast after cast to bring one in to him, but nothing would bite. And when I tried to carry him across the cold stream to watch from the other bank, I slipped again, baptizing him in the cold, glacial-fed water. Rather than bring the fish to him, I had brought him to the fish.

But his interest in fishing has continued, so much so that early this summer we took a trip into the Southwest Virginia Highlands to fish Bear Creek Lake (for him) and Virginia's premier trout stream, Whitetop Laurel Creek (for me). We started at the stocked lake because the first rule of fishing with kids is that you must catch fish.

By the cold mountain stream that feeds the pond, Sam caught the first fish of the day on a spinner while the cool morning fog hovered above the lake surface. He caught four more trout that day, using a combination of spinners, worms, and "fire balls" or salmon eggs. He tried my fly rod too. We had practiced casting, but his always looked more like the whip one does to dry off the fly. Still, he could whip out a cast and land a bluegill by watching them rise and setting the hook in their obliging mouths. But trout are different, finicky. He was beginning to sense that.

＊ ＊ ＊

To catch them, he first fished the cold holes where the stream joins the lake and the trout lie in waiting, watching food drift downstream.

Once that section was exhausted, he moved on to the neck of the lake and base of the stream, and then the stream itself. From a gravel bar, he could cast upstream and dangle a worm in the eddies or let his salmon egg float downstream. He was learning to read the water and not spook the fish. He would lie low and quiet and watch. And then he would move upstream to where a hemlock trunk crossed the water and fish the shade. Patience is what people commonly say you need to fish, and perhaps that's it if all you do is watch your bobber. But persistence is what it takes. If one thing doesn't work, you try another, or you move to a different section of the stream.

The patience is necessary for the parent. Just as I am about to thread my tippet though the eyelet of the fly or in a position to cast—each time I thought I was close to getting my own strike—I am called upon to undo a tangle or change a hook. And when you fish with children, you discover that fishing tangles have their own laws of physics. On a good day, the number of fish we land is greater than the number of trees we catch. The Maclean brothers had to be older than seven when they learned their father's trinity of art, grace, and trout. Trout we know, and art is coming, but grace remains an abstraction. Sam also caught his finger twice that day, but he kept fishing.

Because he likes fishing and he likes fishing talk. "Any luck?" he will gladly shout out to other boats on the New River. "What'd ya catch him on?" When other anglers began showing up at Bear Creek Lake that day, he would gladly point out how many he caught and how, and he would offer his spot. "Over here. There's bluegills." Fishermen like to brag, but they don't much like to share. Since it's my job to tutor him in the finer points of fishing etiquette, I say something.

"What?" he tells me. "I like to give information."

The next day we tried Whitetop Laurel Creek. But first we had to release one of the bluegills he had caught the day before and kept in a bucket. He was hoping to maybe keep it as a pet. "We could build a pond." At dusk at the same lake, some men were tying bells onto their lines. They would toss out the bait and wait for a ring in the dark, as if the fish come to you out of a dream. That's why we were heading to the wilder stream, so he could understand wild fish and the proper respect for the hunt.

He had his single-hook spinner, some "trout magnets," and I my flies. We fished near each other, but with the roar of the stream echoing through the steep valley, we couldn't communicate, and his mobility was limited. I kept walking back and forth, from my hole to his, just to hear what he wanted to say. I thought I could put him in places where he could fish from the bank and I could wade out to undo tangles and snags, but you can't fish White-top Laurel that way. Wild fish are too smart, and so we didn't get far.

Whitetop Laurel Creek is a favorite of Virginia anglers because it's wild and yet easy to get to. The Appalachian Trail follows and crosses it, and the Virginia Creeper Trail, an old railroad bed converted to a bike trail, parallels the stream into the town of Damascus. We biked it one day this fall with the whole family, and at Bridge 33 we stopped. The creek turns a sharp right before it passes under the old railroad trestle, and there in the deep pool just beyond the bridge pillars, we could see seven, eight, thirteen dark forms holding fast in the current. He had caught enough fish this summer to feel the tightening at that sight. For Nick Adams it would have been "all the old feeling," but for Sam it was still new.

For a month and a half he talked about it until the bridge gained the force of myth, as if bathed in a special quality of light that would cause so many fish to be there. So to the mythical Bridge 33.

* * *

We brought our bikes and rode the trail upstream and upgrade with fly rods only. But first we started in Taylor's Valley, because we had seen fish there too. That morning we saw them again, and one looked to be about a foot and a half.

"Dad, look at that one. He's huge!"

"He's a lunker," I admit.

I worked upstream of the bridge, and Sam tried a copper nymph from the bridge itself. I expected few results before we got to 33, but he hooked one and shouted with ecstasy. His rod horseshoed, bent in half, and he reeled furiously. "I got one! I got one!" But he pulled too hard. When the fish came out of the water—its presence made sparkling and clear—it spit out the hook.

"That's a half," he said, disheartened, after the practice we have of counting fish we almost land.

"It was a nice one," I say, trying to be encouraging and hoping the mood won't be spoiled for the trip upstream.

* * *

We try everything when we arrive, but there's no easy place to reach the water. The right bank is steep, forcing a left-handed cast. From the left, there's an overhanging hemlock and some wires to duck under. We try under the bridge first, hiding behind the pillars and letting both wet and dry flies drift downstream. We try together and apart. Eventually, one of us is up on the bridge, guiding casts and placement, scouting the fly, with the other underneath trying to wish them out.

"A little to the left. To the right. There. Leave it there. He's looking. He's interested. Hold it. He's not taking it. Try again."

When Sam puts his line in the guy wires of the bridge piers, he has had it: "Who are the fishing gods? Because I hate them." His lower lip juts out and he pouts: "And I hate fishing." But he knows it's not true. He's a good enough fisherman that he just hates not catching fish.

On the way back to the car, we try a few more spots but have little success. But we keep trying, and pretty soon the day has gone. On the way home, we drive over the bridge in Taylor's Valley. "Let's count that one," he says, dejectedly. As he learns to fly fish, the warp of disappointment mingles with the woof of expectation—of what lies at the next bridge. What you try one day may or may not work the next. Some days the fishing gods smile upon you, and some days you slip and make a terrible mess. But he has felt that electrifying struggle on the end of his fly rod, a feeling better than any mounted fish or pet bluegill, and he knows he will be back.

field guides

THE GREEN, VINYL-COVERED *North American Reptiles and Amphibians* published by the Audubon Society was probably the first, followed closely by the yellow *North American Butterflies*. Both are thumb-worn, their color plates pulling away from the binding. We added them to those my wife and I already owned: the brown *North American Trees* and the *Field Guide to the Birds of North America* by the National Geographic Society. They put out a good My First Pocket Guide series, and we have some for mammals, reptiles, and fish. An older friend cleaning out her bookshelves gave us the *Golden Guide* to pond life and one for wildflowers, "full-color, easy-to-use," and we had to get a *Birds of the World* when we lived in Europe.

The modern field guide was created by Roger Tory Peterson. His seminal and succinctly titled *Guide to the Birds*, with its clear illustrations, revolutionized birding when it appeared in 1934. Among our Peterson's favorites are *Eastern Forests* and *Eastern Birds' Nests*. Now there are field guides to rocks and minerals, beetles and dragonflies.

We have Bigelow's *Mushroom Pocket Field-Guide* and the *Field Guide to Grasshoppers, Katydids, and Crickets of the United States*. For times when the field is seen from the car, we purchased *The Book of Field and Roadside: Open-Country Weeds, Trees, and Wildflowers of Eastern North America*. Most guides are handy enough to be taken into the field, with pictures organized by family, color, shape, location, or other descriptors to aid in identification.

Spot a blue flower and look in the blue section; mushrooms are organized by gill, tube, teeth, and coral families. Tree books are sometimes organized by shape, toothed or lobed in the case of deciduous, needled or scaled in that of conifers, and they will have sections on cones, balls, nuts, seeds, and fruit. Butterfly books are a mix of color (sulphurs, whites, blues), shape (swallowtail, angelwings), pattern (metalmarked, checkered, eyespots), and family (skippers, both folded-winged and spread). Field guides help put a name to that which we are seeing, allowing us to further know and value a species or just to satisfy a curiosity. But sometimes what we see we cannot find in the book; sometimes we need someone else to show us. "If a child is to keep alive his inborn sense of wonder," wrote Rachel Carson, "he needs the companionship of at least one adult who can share it, rediscovering with him the joy, excitement, and mystery of the world we live in."

If I stumble upon a bird or a plant I don't know, I may need to ask someone. And though field guides can tell you what you are looking at, they don't always tell you where to look.

* * *

The first time we met Rudi Woykowski, he was giving a talk on reptiles and amphibians at our local library, waving a bandaged and swollen hand. He had been bitten by a timber rattlesnake the day before while trying to keep six coiled ones away from his dog. One snake put two puncture wounds in his right hand. Rudi felt the neurotoxins almost immediately, and within ten minutes he was lights out. Rudi is thin, of average height, and on that day he was lucky to be hiking with a friend at least a half-foot taller and fifty pounds heavier than he. His taller friend carried Rudi on his shoulder back to the truck and drove him to the local hospital. They then airlifted Rudi to the University of Virginia Medical Center, where he was given twenty-three vials of antivenin. The next day he was at our local library, his cotton sacks ("allows them to relax and breathe") writhing with snakes, his plastic containers full of turtles and frogs. Two were duct-taped shut—a copperhead and a timber rattler. No hard feelings. The show must go on.

He gives the afternoon audience of wide-eyed, restless youngsters a few rules: you can't poke or touch, and you must stay out of the masking-tape runway. "They're not used to having this many people look at them."

Rudi's main goal is to educate people—especially kids—about the reptiles and amphibians in their region, and to give his audience the knowledge of how to interact with them. He gives lectures at local libraries and to the Boy Scouts. He also runs Rudi's Reptile Removal. If you have a snake under your porch and you want "animal friendly extraction" (says his business card), call Rudi. I know. I once had a corn snake, a family pet, under there. Rudi's a reptile expert, and I'm a decent carpenter, so we had several floorboards removed—giving light to the dusty world between house and foundation, Rudi slithering through dirt on elbows and knees. He found no snake this time, but he saw our rubber raft. "Anytime you want to take that thing down the New River Gorge, let me know." Always up for an adventure is our Rudi.

He brings out a bullfrog first, talks about the way it uses its eyes to eat. Their blinking motion helps move their food back. "I have a bullfrog," one youngster says. Rudi nods but keeps moving. Then a wood frog, able to survive being frozen in winter ice. He brings out a box turtle, which seals itself up—"I caught one of them once"—and a musk turtle, which eats crawdads. Then the snapping turtle, amid gasps from the audience, its feet clawing and its head lunging for Rudi's hands. "Notice that the snapping turtle's neck reaches back only to about halfway on its shell," Rudi relates. "If you would hold one, you hold it here, firmly." Rudi clutches it midway back on the shell as it wriggles and arches its head. On one of our first trips into the field with Rudi, he walked into the boggy end of the pond with water sandals, toes exposed, trying to flush out same snapping turtles.

Hands go up. "What's your question?" he asks one enthusiastic toddler. "That's not a question," he has to say, at least three times. There's some discipline that goes on at Rudi's sessions: we have business to do, learning to make happen—pay attention or you could get hurt. But it's not hard to imagine the display table tipping over, snakes spilling out of their containers and slipping through the stacks, kids screaming for the doors. "What does it eat?" someone finally says. And another, "Does it bite?" Both questions now become standard fare for each species. "It won't try to hurt you unless you threaten it."

We meet up with Rudi again one day where he's more at home, out in the field, near where the Appalachian Trail crosses Craig Creek. He has his "water skeeter" in his truck, a single-person pontoon boat good for fishing. "Probably caught twenty-five fish near McCoy Falls."

Before we start, he shows the group some of the species we might see, all of them "rescued" from people's yards and kept in temporary captivity. He brings out a king snake, a milk snake, and a garter. The garter produces a musky smell. "You won't enjoy a sandwich for days if you get it on you." This one just gave birth to forty young. He helps us tell the difference between the black rat and the more slender racer, the latter with a disposition against being handled. And he brings out one of his favorites, the hognose, which eats mostly the American toad, using its front teeth to deflate the toad's puffed-up air sacs. "What eats it?" one kid asks, a variation on the line of questioning. Finally, he shows us a northern copperhead and the main attraction, a timber rattlesnake, both secured safely in glass tanks but exhibits of what we are there to see live in the field. He also shows us his snake tools, a hook and a squeezer. He prefers to use the former, because the snake will relax, like it is slithering over a branch, but may need to use the latter, which feels predatory to the snake.

One reason we are here, says Rudi, is so we can observe the snakes in their own environment, where they shelter, and where they are less defensive. "If I do my job right and stay relaxed, the snake will relax, might even crawl over my foot." "When I got bit," snake whisperer Rudi adds, "I lunged."

He delivers all this in a somewhat sober voice, as if to make clear that this trip is about education and not amusement. There will be no "crikey" or "have a go at that." The death of the Crocodile Hunter was a sad day in our house. For all his showmanship, he looked at nature like a kid. He was duly criticized for holding his infant son while feeding a crocodile, but he offered a good response: that he held his son at safe distance, and that if people didn't take some risks near animals, we wouldn't sense their wonder. Without that, we might not learn enough to know how to live with them.

All this is cold comfort as we walk up a rocky area under a power line and my son bends over shoulder to shoulder with Rudi to help him turn over rocks and logs. In the summer, female timber rattlers will migrate away from their den, especially to open, rocky ledges where temperatures can be higher, while the males seem to prefer cooler, thicker woods where the forest canopy is closed. I am looking around to see if anyone is big enough to carry me off the mountain, but today we find only a worm snake, small and resembling a worm, and several fence lizards warming on the power company's stumps. Just a month earlier Rudi found five copperheads and three rattlesnakes in the same spot, the charismatic and scary species the Crocodile Hunter favors

Sam is disappointed, but he learns what looking for snakes is really like. The TV shows do not present the hunt for species, only the highlights, but now we know where to look—and how.

* * *

When I meet Clyde Kessler one day in the nearby park, he is already waist deep in the meadow, following a swarthy skipper, a brown butterfly with pale veins on the wing. He has also turned up a skipper of the variety *sachem*, an Algonquin term for chief or leader, curious title for a little tawny-orange butterfly. Clyde wears field glasses hanging from his neck and resting below his beard. If he doesn't know what he is looking at, he has brought along his field guides, located in another case swinging by his side. But most of the time Clyde knows what he is looking at.

As we walk, Clyde points out the song of the wood thrush and also that of a towhee—"drink your tea." He points out the autumn olive in the field, an invasive species, "another one of those great ideas gone bad." Walk with Clyde and an otherwise ordinary landscape awakens with life. "There's the great blue skimmer right in front of you. They're not very common in this park." A step farther, "Hear the indigo bunting. There's the male, and the female sounds like she's over in that next tree."

Clyde has been learning the names of the species around him for some forty-five years since he was a five-year-old in Franklin County, Virginia, known for its preachers but especially its moonshiners. "I had both in my family. They didn't always get along."

"My family thought it was wonderful," he said, about his search to know the names of critters and his bringing some of them home. "By the time I was thirteen they were getting worried." His father showed him a nest of some common yellowthroats—peewee bird to the Kesslers. "It was all over from there." Clyde had developed an interest in all things that fly, not just birds but what he calls "aerial plankton," the stuff birds eat.

At a citywide dedication of a new birding platform, the mayor spoke, the economic development person talked, the leader of a citizens group said a few words, and then Clyde, reluctant Clyde. Rather than speak, he asked us to listen, to be silent for two minutes. I recognized three species (one a crow), but Clyde heard eleven. In a five-minute walk before we started, he heard or saw twenty-seven, including the Baltimore orioles that finished sewing their hanging-nest baskets from sycamores. Of the 212 species known to have been seen in the New River Valley, Clyde has seen 205. His most exotic? The glossy ibis.

I was walking with him because the following day I was taking my son's second-grade class on a field trip through the park, and though I didn't think second-graders could stump me, I wanted to be sure I knew what I was talking about. A walk with Clyde was the dry run. "It starts when they're young," he said. Down near the creek we see a jack-in-the-pulpit with an exuberant jack, but this species is unisexual or monoecious, a word I'll spare the kids, though it can also change gender, something too tempting not to share.

On another day, my kids and I join him on a butterfly walk sponsored by the Parks and Recreation Department. Clyde points out the cabbage white with black spots, fluttering among the flowers, the wild indigo dusky wing on host crown vetch, the great spangled fritillary, the orange sulphur, a viceroy, and an eastern-tailed blue. Of this he relates how it has an orange spot and a dark outline on its folded wings. The wings have "tails" that look like antennae, and the spot an eye—both ward off predators. "It's called tricks," Clyde says, with a gleam. I can see his excitement, still dormant in my kids. We also spot his favorite, the northern metalmark, and we see up close its spectacular splashes of silver on dark-orange wings.

That same day, he tells us the difference between dragon- and damselflies. Dragon, for the most part, keep their wings out like a plane. Damselflies can fold them up parallel to their body. I've had them backward for a long time. Of the former, we see the common whitetail; among the latter, the eastern red and variable dancer. I've had other things wrong too. What I thought was Queen Anne's lace was really cow parsnip, a member of the carrot parsley family, and what I thought was Carolina phlox (five petals) was really the four-petaled dame's rocket.

Clyde got interested in natural history in part because of words.

He's a past president of the Appalachian Writers Association and an accomplished poet. He earned a master's in linguistics because he "loved words and the way the relate to each other." He also loves live things, and the way they interact.

We see a great spangled on some dog poop. "Only the males get nectar from there," Clyde notes, with a little mischief. "Maybe it says something about men." We hear a gnatcatcher, but wouldn't know it was there if Clyde hadn't pointed it out. Then a broad-winged hawk soars above us. Finally, something my kids and I recognize.

Clyde's knowledge is both encyclopedic and folkloric, covering both the scientific names and the ones he knew as a boy, the names his grandparents gave to the "critters" and herbal plants of Franklin County. Native clematis is leather flower. A green heron is a "shitepoke," because it may crap on your head. "My father used to say that if you got too close, they'd bomb it on you," he says, with a smile and a laugh. Towhees are joereens, for the sound they make, and a flicker is a yellow hammer, for the work they do. A pileated woodpecker is simply a wood hen, for the way it cackles in the forest, and common wood nymph, northern pearly-eye, and silver-spotted skipper were all called Daisy Kates. He called the summer tanager a crestless cardinal: "If I didn't know it, I would make up my own name," he says, with a shrug.

We see Clyde again one summer night, giving a presentation in the park, part of a summer naturalist series. He shows pictures of the flying things, moving through birds and butterflies. Some we are familiar with from Clyde's walks. Some are new, like tawny emperor, host hackberry. "You can't get rid of it. It likes sweat." When he gets to the dragon- and damselflies, he's arrived at "my favorite group of bugs." Green darner, swamp darner, magnificent. Variable dancer.

Ebony jewelwing. And the common whitetail and eastern red, both skimmers.

"Best thing to do is get out and look, folks." "Books are supplements," says Kessler. "Your main tools are these," he says, pointing to his eyes, "and these," tugging on his ear. Too often kids' eyes are seduced by the flicker of screens, their ears plugged up with headphones. Being able to put names to plants and creatures gives kids something to be proud of, an accomplishment they have earned. "Attention," writes Mary Oliver, "is the beginning of devotion."

The way Clyde or any naturalist looks at the world begins with a name but then moves on to the relationships, the context, the role in the ecosystem of the thing. After he can name *what* it is, he might notice *where*, unless where it is helps name it. Sycamores grow near the creeks, preferring "wet feet." Different species thrive in the shrub, understory, and canopy layers, and they come out at different times. What he sees is determined by *when* he sees it, including season, weather, and time of day. We often see box turtles after rain, snakes in the morning sun. Clyde thinks about *who* are its predators, its prey, and *how* it has adapted. Species with eyes on the sides of their heads are usually prey, watching for what could sneak up. Species with eyes set deep in their heads, owls and hawks, are predators, scanning the ground below. Others will mimic or "play tricks." Finally, he moves on to *why* the species is there. Is it native? Does it have some relationship to the host plant?

You won't learn what Clyde knows in an afternoon—"There's the alternate song of the Acadian flycatcher"—but you might catch on to the way he looks.

On the way back from our walk, he points out a titmouse family in a locust. "They've got hungry kids." And then he stops, listening: a yellow-breasted chat, a migratory bird visiting from South America. The chat is a mimic, and Kessler and a Virginia Tech professor think it mimics the cry of monkeys. So we have monkeys in Wildwood Park after all. Who needs Jeff Corwin?

"You know this place really well," says Sam. "I want to get a map of this place," he adds, thinking of one that would include not just topography but the details Kessler knows.

"You can't make any money at it," Clyde says. "Same with these species. You can't save them unless there's money in it."

Maybe we can't save species without money. Local development keeps pushing farther into the mountains where we roam for timber rattlesnakes. But imagine if every kid had one of those maps in their heads, of not only where they are but what inhabits that landscape. Imagine if they knew plants and animals the way they knew brand names and logos, if they knew mountains the way they know malls. They would feel like full participants of the landscapes they inhabit, happily roaming the ridges and creeks in a world that needs their attentiveness. If they only had a map of this place.

swimming hole

I BEGAN THE SUMMER with two simple goals: grow a garden and find a place to swim, a place to cool down and clean up after hoeing and weeding, a watery area to call our own, a swimming hole. We live on the New River, one of the oldest rivers, flowing north out of the Carolina mountains and through Virginia on its way to the Ohio. The New is the cleanest mainstem river in Virginia by all accounts, but rarely will you see people swimming in it. They mostly paddle and fish, sometimes tube on this stretch, but few swimmers, people out swimming, taking a leisurely and refreshing dip.

I grew up in a town on the Delaware, also a river town, but with a whole river culture. The houses all face the water, high up on the bank. And down on the river, people have boat docks, platforms from which to swim. In Radford, the river almost seems an afterthought to town planners. In some places, one has to traverse six lanes of railroad tracks to get to it. At fifty-eight-acre Bisset Park, with about a half-mile of river bank, there's no official access.

I swam in the Delaware River, bathed in it—it cleansed me. Used to keep a bar of soap on a barrel under the dock. My friend Michael and I would try to jump in earlier each spring, later and later each fall. I made it to November once, when the river was low and clear. Jumped in once late March, the river breathtakingly cold, bragging-rights cold.

To most people, even swimming in the river was crazy. "You swim in that river?" A common view is that rivers are merely cesspools, sewage transport. Some of them are. According to the EPA, 40 percent of America's rivers are not clean enough to swim in. But some of them, thanks to the Clean Water Act, are cleaner than ever. Fresh water, cool, clean water, running downstream from some forested hillside that collects and distributes rain.

But something else keeps people out of the river too. David Sobel defines ecophobia as a fear of the natural world but also its deterioration. Because there's so much bad news about the environment, children disassociate themselves from it, like a victim of abuse "cutting themselves off from the pain." For Sobel, children fear nature too because so much of their learning about it is abstract. They study rainforests, for example, that are far removed from home. All kids really need to feel comfortable in the natural world, says Sobel, is "modeling by a responsible adult," contact with nature, and an adult to help them form a relationship.

If there is something like ecophobia, perhaps it manifests itself most often in and around natural watercourses. I have heard more than one kid confuse crayfish with crabs, and refuse to go in the water because of either. They ask if there are sharks in the river or other creatures that bite, such as water moccasins (found only miles south and east of here). No toe-eating bass, though a rabid otter did bite (nay maul, in her words) a woman this summer in upstream Claytor Lake (where the New is impounded by a dam), a story the newspaper felt worthy of the front page: "Deranged Otter Attacks Pregnant Woman." "It was like a scene from *Jaws*," noted one witness.

A friend once told me that she swims only when she can see bottom. "Who knows what could be down there," she tells me. "I need to see my feet." When I touted the cleanliness of the New River in class, a student said: "That river? But it's not blue." The paint on the bottoms of swimming pools and the spring break brochures had convinced her of water's hue. Swimming in the river is so aberrant that my friend Mark was mistaken for committing suicide by drowning. He waded in to cool his shin splints after a run, and a woman came waving and hollering across the grass from the parking lot, "Don't do it! Don't!"

* * *

I have set two more ongoing goals: to help my daughter forge a bond with the natural world and develop a sense of physical competence and adventure, both readily fostered in boys but overlooked in girls as a basis for a forming a strong, independent self. She will often have to swim against the currents (so hard for some girls to fight) of front-page glossies: how to be chic, how to fit in, how to be completely anxious about who you are. Older brother Sam would rather fish, but six-year-old Elliot acts like a fish, wriggling with delight whenever in or around water.

She has mostly avoided the fear of the watery world beneath the surface, that water horror of traps, hidden depths, old rusty cars, and weeds waiting to grab hold of a leg or foot. Admittedly, sometimes something brushes my leg, or I touch something squishy and I move fast. But it's always nothing, just me twitching. For the most part, kids get over the ick factor fast, rolling up the seaweed into balls or bombs, draping it over their hair to make crowns or the locks of Medusa. Part of the fun of swimming in a river is overcoming that fear, knowing that we can ride that wave.

With the New, the fear of natural water is compounded by the fact that we live several miles downstream from a hydroelectric dam. The water is thought to rise suddenly, producing a surge, even a wave. At a picnic, I once approached our mayor about the possibility of an access area in the park, a Bisset Beach, asking him to leave questions of liability aside for the moment. "I don't know. That river rises awful fast." He couldn't leave liability aside.

It doesn't help that the river is rumored to have been called "The River of Death." I can find mention of this name only in Patricia Givens Johnson's *New River Early Settlement*, which notes that the "Indians of West Virginia" called it this, but there was no West Virginia then, not even a Virginia. The Shawnee are said to have called it Keninskeha, which means "river of evil spirits," and in the New River Gorge of West Virginia, the river is much more dangerous. An almost countervailing myth, were it not historically accurate, concerns the story of Mary Draper Ingles, kidnapped by the Shawnee and taken all the way to the Ohio. To find her way home, for forty-three days she would "follow the river," the title of a historical novel by James Thom.

The river can certainly rise fast in flood conditions, sometimes flooding the park and the freshman parking lots near Radford University. But no one I know swims during (or after) storms. From April 15 to October 15 the Claytor Hydro Plant performs an annual "run of the river" release, a levelized operation "designed to accommodate recreational needs and activities downstream from the dam on New River." The U.S. Geological Survey hosts a website of real-time data, revealing the discharges and gauge height of the New. In August the graph spikes twice a day, enough to raise the tailwater elevation at most half a foot, but mostly it levels off, a consistent 1,730 feet above sea level, making few waves.

Other than from heavy rains, the river rises once a year. On October 15, American Electric Power performs a "drawdown," lowering the lake elevation so property owners can make repairs to their docks. On that day, Radford residents have reported a bubble of up to four feet high. Sheriff Mark Armentrout tells me he has ridden it some thirty river miles to Pearisburg on a jet ski.

I don't mean to downplay the dangers of the New, for every year someone drowns in it. But my kids have picked up on the erroneous perception that you can be walking along in shallow water and all of sudden be sucked into a deep hole, as if there were an undertow in a river. When the depth of a river changes fast, its underwater secret is most often revealed on the surface, in the form of eddies, swirls, or bubbles. These and the swift water of certain places, such as at the gorge in West Virginia, or flood conditions, are to be avoided. My job as parent is to help them read the water, test the current, and assess the risk.

The search for a swimming hole has taken on some urgency because my city has closed down the only public pool. Citing maintenance costs and neglect, they closed the pool in the park overlooking the river, filling it in with soil and covering it over with grass.

This is the second pool the city has closed. We had one made in the valley of another park, Wildwood Park, with water fed by a

New River tributary. The December 20, 1928, *Radford News-Journal* said that "for adults and for children alike, provision for adequate recreation is important," and so they endorsed a new pool. It was to be "a new place of assemblage, where people of various groups will come together, play together." The pool opened on Independence Day in 1929 and averaged more than four hundred people a day despite the fact that the cold creek-fed water and shade from nearby steep hillsides kept the water frigid.

But in 1964, citing neglect and maintenance costs, the city closed the pool. In 1964 a series of cultural changes were also sweeping through the South. On July 6, 1964, the *News-Journal* carried this report. "Integration came to the city of Radford Sunday at the public swimming pool. A family of Negroes requested entrance at the gate of the pool. Their money was refused, but they entered the pool." City officials did not comment. In 1977 the pool was filled with dirt, covered over with grass.

There's a swim club nearby, a private pool—chlorine sterile—but it requires us to buy stock to belong. I'd rather put my stock in the river, even if it means my kids have poor swimming form: they are doggie paddlers and nose holders, clueless around a diving board, even more so about the preteen strutting and towel snapping at pool's edge.

So we head down to the river, where no one is refused, cross the grass of the soccer field and nearby playground, kids (can we come?) and their parents (can you do that?) looking on, past the NO SWIM-MING sign (merely for liability), to a small opening in the trees. We climb down the roots, the rebar of the river bank, stay away from the poison ivy, and drape our shirts on nearby branches. With a whiff of the river silt, I am a boy again floating down the Delaware.

Then we walk out the gravelly bottom (old sneakers help), past the shade of the leaners, and release our bodies to the current, let the gentle flow caress us, wedge toes on the rocky riverbed. No need to fear hidden feet: we can look down and spot skipping stones when the water is waist-high.

There's a spot under the railroad bridge with a bedrock bottom, ideal for bridge pillars, also good for swimming holes. But in the water we see railroad tie spikes and tie plates, and then hear the hoot and rumble of the train overhead. This spot is also used for beer drinking and fishing (ubiquitous bait cups and Eagle Claw packages), probably at the same time, and so feels a little junky— the vista is also closed off by rough-cut stone pillars and an iron bridge above, a rust rain when the locomotive passes over. Another spot looks good from the bike trail, but the current is a little swift, the rocky beach too filled with glass and pottery shards. In another, near the islands upstream from town, and the fish weir believed to be left by Indians—just up from the remains of Ingles Ferry—Elliot jumps out of the canoe. One leg sinks thigh-high in mud, the other remains in the boat, it slowly pushing away from shore.

* * *

In pursuit of a good swimming hole, we've even expanded the search to a two-hundred-mile radius from home. There are many good ones in this mountain region. All you need is some running water, some seclusion, and a depression in the nearby streambed causing or eliciting joy. To narrow down the search, we are aided by the Internet, specifically swimminghole.org, a not-for-profit website focusing on "moving, fresh water spots . . . especially beautiful or fun for swimming."

On Memorial Day weekend, we try our first, Blue Bend in West Virginia, with nearby camping and a "family friendly" designation. Elliot and I swim out to a gravel bar and then across another deep stretch to the other side. Then we hold hands and run until we fall in the water, stroke back to the other side, and repeat. We kick up silt, bits of mica that the minnows swim after, swimming with us.

The next day, we go to a more remote hole, nearby Hippy Hole ("bathing suits may be optional"). The information is always anecdotal: "Very shortly you will ford the creek and in a short distance more you will come to a trail junction. Go left and when the trail comes back to Anthony's Creek and makes a sharp bend left you will be at Hippy." When we arrive, others are camping there (damn hippies), so we wade downstream and find eddies. Cold mountain water tumbles though the tall canyon on the first warm day of spring. We sit in thrones, impressions in the rock, and let the stream surround our feet, legs, waist.

Next to Devil's Bathtub, "not really close to anywhere," the mile-and-a-half trail takes you through a luxuriant forest, up an old logging road framed by laurels and hemlock, the forest floor damp with rattlesnake orchid (*Goodyera pubescens*) and many mushrooms, some rose-red and some that look like coral. The walk feels like a quest through some forest primeval, a river Styx, but nothing satanic about it. After many stream crossings, the cascades grow in size and frequency until we arrive at a crystal-clear pool, a small waterfall crashing into it, ledges on both sides that could be benches for Naiads.

Above it, there is a section of rock scooped out by water, in the

shape of a tub, water tripping over bedrock steps and swirling currents into the tub, only the water is not warm like a bath. It is cold,
bone-tingling cold, but so invigorating. The rocks there are moss-
covered, slippery, and we try to slide on them, but no waterslide
exists in nature: one is always reminded that what one's bottom
bumps over is rock. A guy we meet on his horse says he hasn't been
back there since he was a kid: "That water will take your breath
away, buddy." We also see a copperhead on the way up that takes
our breath away.

Then to the nearby Cascades, a lacy sixty-foot waterfall at the end
of a two-mile hike. We go on the hottest day of the year, a 100-degree
day, with three other neighborhood kids, and meet a man who drove
two and a half hours from Charlottesville to get here. He swims out
in the deep water, but the kids hug the shore, jump off small rocks,
hide behind the waterfall curtain, laughter echoing over the rocks.
"This has to be the best swimming hole," the man says. "I'll be back."
So will we. We try Dismal Falls, but it's too close to the road and
too full of trash: tampons and toilet paper, bottle caps and butts, a
pair of sunglasses hanging from a knot in a tree, a rubber raft. One
wonders what would happen if the falls weren't named Dismal? If
the county wasn't Bland (and if there wasn't a six-hundred-person
correctional facility nearby)?

Still, it is a good place to explore. While Sam fishes for minnows,
using the smallest fly I have, Elliot says, "Follow me Dad," and I am
taken aback by the reversal of our roles. She balances across a log
bridge over the upper creek, then up a trail under the rhodies, back
into the creek and up some rocks, a steep crag, exploring, climbing,
adventuring. A good swimming hole, after all, is made by rocks
moving and misbehaving long ago.

Then to Wolf Creek in Narrows ("Narz" to some), where the New River narrows, and their swimming hole "the boom," because it was a log boom. Elliot jumps from the platform on the far shore.

Mostly, though, it's back to our place on the New, not really a hole since it's not circular, unless all rivers are holes in the ground. On summer nights we ride our bikes down to cool off before bed. Usually, it's just us kids, but once it was filled with people. Perry Slaughter, the associate pastor of Valley Harvest Ministries, told me that baptism is symbolic of being "buried with Christ and rising to something new," a public declaration of faith. The church has a dunking tank on-site, but that day they decided to take it to the New, making their ceremony even more public. As we approached, we became mesmerized by their song: the phrase "take me to the water" repeated, the word "water" rising in pitch until "take me to the waaaaaterrrrr," wait a beat, "to be baptized."

Just upstream from this spot, under what is now Claytor Lake, was a town called Dunkard's Bottom. A "dunkard" was a term of derision for people who were "dunkers," German Baptists who practiced a trine (as in Trinity) immersion baptism.

The second verse crescendos to "none but the riiiigtheous," and then trails off to "shall see God." We see a lot of omniscient creatures at the river, mortal spirits. We see the periwinkle blue dancer, a damselfly, skim across the surface. Great blue herons glide toward landings, sometimes squawking, and belted kingfishers dart near the shoreline, often rattling, like a heavy fishing reel. There are always ducks down there, and orioles and bluebirds in spring. Young, acrobatic swallows play by dropping a feather for a playmate to catch below, practice for hunting insects. Like bluebirds, tree swallows are secondary cavity nesters, preferring to use an existing nest rather than create or excavate a new one. So are we with our swimming holes.

In *Historic Springs of the Virginias*, Stan Cohen documents about seventy-five healing springs, spas, and baths, all "founded on the premise that their waters, no matter what type, could cure common diseases at a time when medical science really could not do much for patients." Neither cholera nor yellow fever were common in the mountains, the former because it existed mostly downstream, the latter because it was mostly found on the warmer seacoast. There was Yellow Sulphur and White Sulphur Springs (and a blue and a red one too), Hot Springs and Warm Springs (both still there), Sparkling Springs and Healing Springs. Often these were places for the elite (in some cases still are), but some also bottled their water, sold it as an elixir, an elusive fountain of youth.

We don't drink the water here on the New when we swim (although our drinking water comes from it), but we do find healing, youthful properties in it. After Elliot dives under she emerges again on top, breaking the surface of the water, pulling the wet hair from her eyes, wiping the beads from her eyelashes. We go down together, keep our eyes open to look at one another—our hair floating up toward the light—until one of us makes a face and the other releases a burst of bubbly laughter. We come to the river to cool down, but I hope this water also provides a spark in my daughter: an immutable kinship with nature, a connection to her home waters, the wisdom to overcome fear.

At the onset of evening, summer almost over, I take the kids to the river. Elliot and I swim out to the middle, past where her mom likes us to be. She asks to jump from my shoulders, then kicks away by herself and comes back to me, her dock, a life buoy, a balding guy on his tiptoes standing in the middle of the New. One day we will swim to the other side. We started this year in early May. Next year we will shoot for April. We could keep swimming this year through fall. She and I have made a pact to swim together anywhere, anytime. Tonight, she refuses to get out, though I'm shivering on shore. "No way. Swimming is my destiny!" School will start soon and she will sit in straight, dry rows, but for now she swims, knowing that it's safe to go in the water.

false cape

"TICKS AND BITING INSECTS are numerous, insect repellent and sunscreen are a must. Beware, too, of eastern cottonmouths, a poisonous snake also known as a water moccasin." I had been warned by the website that camping was "not recommended for young children or inexperienced campers," but we were experienced, and why should young children be deprived of one of the last undisturbed coastal environments on the East Coast? We had been to the beach, to the Jersey Shore and the Outer Banks, but I had hoped for a camping and coastal experience outside of an air-conditioned condo.

False Cape State Park, a mile-wide barrier spit between Back Bay and the Atlantic Ocean, earned its name because it resembled Cape Henry to early sailors, the entrance to Chesapeake Bay twenty miles to the north. But rather than a safe harbor from the turbulent Atlantic, boats were lured into treacherous shallow waters, where they often ran aground. We would be able to see remains of one of these shipwrecks off the coast during low tide, walk trails that lead to spooky gravesites and settlement ruins, in a natural area so pristine no vehicles are permitted.

The only access is by foot, bike, or boat, some six miles to the Barbour Hill Boat Dock and the primitive campsite we had reserved on Sandy Point. The plan was to leave early in the morning, drive four hours to Virginia Beach, all the way down Sandpiper Road to our put-in at Little Island City Park. There, we would load the canoe and spend the afternoon paddling through the Back Bay, a wildlife refuge, taking in the sand dunes, maritime forests, freshwater marshes, and shoreline birds. But I had taken a wrong turn somewhere crossing the Blue Ridge on the way out to the coastal plains, and our drive was more like six hours. My credibility with the crew had been badly wounded, and as we piled in the tents, cooler, dry bags, and fishing gear in the late afternoon, they were getting restless. How far is our campsite? Where are we going? When *will* we be there?

The saltwater was new to our canoe, and though she had carried us through many freshwater rapids, she wasn't so accustomed to the steady rolling waves left by boat wakes, nor up to tracking in the bay's wind. The effect of river rapids is mostly fore and aft, but this motion was side to side, and my paddle-partner up front, a landlubber from Ohio, with her two life-jacketed treasures tucked in between the thwarts, was not feeling comfortable. A six-mile canoe trip on our river is about a two-hour paddle, if that, depending on stops for lunch and swimming, but an hour into our bay trip I saw no recognizable markers, nor easy places to pull over for a break. The kids helped paddle some, but they couldn't get in sync with each other's strokes, clanking the wooden blades. When they alternated sides, they forgot to switch hands, the wrong one on the top. Each reedy cove we pursued went nowhere. A dragonfly hovered in the silent, salty air.

Sam: "How can we camp on these islands?"

Elliot: "How can we swim in this murky water?"

The flash of a long, silvery fish darting by the boat did nothing to ease the tension. Shark? Barracuda? Finally, around a bend in one of the marshes, we saw a weathered clapboard building with a flagpole, surely part of our destination, but it was merely the welcome center to the False Cape, where our map began—we had at least another four miles to go. Tired from the drive, cramped from being confined to the rocking boat, we tied to a nearby dock and stretched our legs. Fed up with wrong turns and false capes, my wife left the crew to talk with an authority who could tell us what was really going on. The kids and I stayed with the boat. Sam threw out a line, and Elliot lowered the crab trap. Elliot broke the silence: "Why are we doing this?"

Why, indeed. Though I thought we might still be able to make it, when Catherine came back there was a new captain in charge: turn this ship around.

* * *

Later that summer I wanted to try again, this time on our home waters, up in the headwaters of the New in Ashe County near Jefferson, North Carolina. The twenty-six-plus miles of New River State Park are also designated as a Wild and Scenic River. Even better, according to the website, "Its shallow, gentle waters and mild rapids are perfect for beginners, families and groups." Accused of not disclosing all information on previous journeys, this time I laid out all the distances and dangers. We were ready to try again.

Why? For my part, I've wanted to introduce my family to one of my favorite pastimes, floating a river and absorbing a landscape from the seat of canoe. I took my first long trip when I was about twelve. Some locals joined together to float a section of the Delaware. We were led by Jim Abbott, a.k.a. "River Jim," owner of Abbott's Marine. Jim's shop sold boats and rented canoes, and he liked to mix business with pleasure and get his neighbors out on the river. We could come along for free if my mother brought lunch.

Several years later I started working at Abbott's, helping boaters into their rented canoes on the Delaware and Raritan Canal, telling them which was the back and which the front, showing them how to hold the paddle, and pointing out that if they faced each other, they wouldn't get far. Later, I led trips of my own, driving the van and eventually the blue bus. From inside the store, behind the counter, Jim hung a chart with distances to river towns: Lambertville, Bull's Island, Frenchtown, Upper Black Eddy, Martin's Creek, Dingman's Ferry, Milford, and Hancock at the top. On one trip, the passengers asked me, their guide, if anyone lived on the islands. I told them they were "uninhibited." I meant "habited," but they liked my way better.

During a summer when I worked there, the business my dad was a partner in went belly-up, so there would be no extravagant vacation that year. Instead, we drove upriver midweek with some of Abbott's canoes. For four days we canoed and camped, explored parts of the river that drifted by our house, the river that I viewed from my seat in the dining room, from my bedroom window, and all my journeys home and away. By now I had learned to steer and read the water, to choose the downward-facing "V" between rocks (an upward "V" indicating the location of rocks) not only to avoid tipping but also, as a challenge, even to steer away from scraping.

To do this, I would often point the bow toward a rock, often to the vexation of the front paddler and "eye" of the boat, then steer off it at the last minute, riding the swift, foamy wave forced off the rock's side.

On this canoe trip and others, I picked up a love for maps, particularly the Delaware River Basin Commission's recreation maps, which, in addition to topography and towns, provided channel locations and depths, stream miles and put-in points, and the classifications of rapids. "We have a one-plus coming up and then a two just after the bridge. Map suggests we run it river right." I came to know those towns I stared at on the chart on Abbott's wall, at least how they looked from the river. I recall the monument where the three states—New Jersey, Pennsylvania, and New York—come together near Port Jervis, remember the river being colder and clearer than on our home stretch, the banks steeper and the terrain more wild in places too. I remember it as the best vacation we ever took.

* * *

The plan for the headwaters trip was to put in at the Wagoner Road Access and float our gear down to one of the primitive camp sites. Then, in the morning, we would paddle down to the 221 bridge where an outfitter would bring us back, only eleven miles, only four or five hours. Surely doable in a day. I made sure this time that we didn't take any wrong turns on the way, mainly by involving my wife in the trip's navigation, but that night, as we unpacked the boat and paddles, the sleeping bags and pads, I noticed that the back of the van wasn't quite as cramped as normal. "Did you, by chance, grab the tents?"

They were home in a chest on the porch, but no problem, we'll camp here in the van. In our Volkswagen, a "weekender," the seats fold down and the top pops up, comfortably sleeping four. But then the ranger came around, shooing us on our way. I pleaded and begged with him.

"If I let you stay in the parking lot, this place will be filled with RVs."

"But we're not an RV. That's just a van. No stove or sink."

"The parking lot is for parking, not for sleeping."

It was getting dark, but he didn't budge. And though I was thinking we might make do with our tarp, my wife was already packing up the gear. That night it poured. Why *are* we doing this?

The next morning we were back, rested and ready to run the eleven miles of scenic New. We pushed off from the same access, wondering at how narrow and beautiful this part of the New River was. The banks supported thick hardwoods but also open meadows of bright wildflowers and dense shrubs. The mountains drew in steep and close. We spotted a great blue heron and their prey, our prey too, anticipating a great day of fishing and floating the river.

Eventually we approached our first rapid, a small Class I near the primitive campground where we had originally intended to stay. A large rock to river right extended from shore, a smaller one stood in the middle, and a gravel bar held the left. Beyond the big rock was a deep pool that looked good for fishing. The plan, as I understood it, was to shoot through the two rocks and the one good wave and miss getting hung up in the shallow riffles. So I steered for the middle rock, meaning to turn starboard at the last minute. "*Rick*, where are you going?" Catherine pushed left to miss the rock, and then the stern hit something, and before we knew it we were sideways. I tried to back paddle, told the crew to remain calm, but something seemed to grab our boat and, in a split second, flipped it over. We stepped in only a foot of water, but Elliot's leg was pinned, the force of the river beating down on the bottom of the red boat. I lift our canoe off the garage and car and put it in by myself, but Catherine was the first to hear Elliot's distress, and she grabbed the half-submerged canoe in the way some mothers are said to lift cars when their children are trapped underneath. Meanwhile, I swam for our lunch, bobbing down the rapids in a cooler, and Sam's tackle box, taking on water and slowly sinking, and the various other objects we hadn't bothered to tie down, because surely we wouldn't swamp in this family-friendly fork of the New River. After the screams subsided, we squeezed water out of the drenched, heavy towels, and I scooped out the boat with a coffee cup.

"Nice *job* Dad," said Elliot.

"We should have gone right," added Sam.

"Who wants a soggy sandwich?" offered Catherine.

From the bank, campers asked if we were okay. Watching with them was the ranger from last night. In memory, he is shaking his head.

We survived our first capsize but also learned that, as long as no one is pinned against a rock (move away from the boat), it is not so bad to flip and travel down the river floating with a life jacket and with feet up to kick off of rocks. Nine miles down the river, a storm came in, and we huddled wet under a bridge, and I finally knocked on the door of a nearby home. The occupant was on his day off and was hoping to watch the NASCAR race, and no, he wasn't aware of how much farther because he doesn't canoe, but yes, he would give me a ride to my car.

* * *

We tried again once more, this time close to home. We would put in only six miles upstream and paddle down to some "uninhibited" islands. At the boat ramp, we loaded our gear and tied it down. Then we all paddled through the rapids, on different sides of the boat, the kids scouting rocks, my wife and I communicating about which line to take. And then, after less than a mile, we pulled into our site, the tip of an island with a tree canopy above and sandy, soft river silt on the ground below.

One advantage of canoe camping is that you can bring enough gear (when you don't forget it) to be comfortable, including the cooler with cold drinks. Later that night, we cleaned and cooked some fish Sam had caught, turning them on large skewers over the fire like hot dogs, scooping out the tender cheek meat—the best part, according to Sam's uncles—last of all. Then we cooked blackberry pies with a pie iron. You put fruit and sugar between two buttered pieces of bread, sandwich them between metal plates at the end of a long handle, and turn it in the fire about two minutes a side. You will inevitably burn yourself, either prying the bread off or while swallowing, but nothing tastes better after a day on the water than a dripping hot hobo pie. We watched the sunset over the sparkling rapids and leafy trees and slept to the hum and burble of the water.

I realize now that I should have done this all in reverse, start with the nearby island to gain experience, then to the state park, and graduate with the bay. Like building a fire: first the small pine needles, then the sticks and twigs, and finally the larger limbs and logs. But there's no predicting how a trip will go, even with the proper planning and packing. Canoeists all know that feeling of canoeing down the river, tired shoulders and sore back, looking for a campsite, only to find the one around the bend has been taken and even the one after that. And we can swamp and get rained on. There may be mosquitoes and poison ivy, and the fire, despite the best and most carefully arranged structure, either log cabin or tipi style (an old argument), might not light, so really, why *are* we doing this?

* * *

Part of the answer to Elliot's question lies in the very unpredictability of these excursions: you never know what may happen when you place a paddle into the water and bubbles swirl behind you and the boat glides forward over smooth surface. Because there is a power to a river, one that can pin us to a rock, yes, but also in the way it enters us. We come to know its every bend, its conditions in high and low water, and the towns along the way. We add to the maps the best routes and the sites of our mishaps, the swimming holes and rope swings, the campsites not marked and that no one knows the name of—but us.

Our sixteen-foot canoe was a wedding present, and it has done more to bring us together than the cutlery set or the waffle iron, though it has also given rise to its share of conflict. But the spills and calamities, especially, have become part of family lore, and part of what ties us together. Canoeists always share a boat. One pushes and the other pulls, but they must work together, giving directions but allowing for mistakes. We can be cold, wet, and tired yet still be glad.

I ask Elliot about canoe camping again this summer, and she free-associates: "Terrible. Nightmares. Terrible nightmares. Storms. Tipping over. Trapped by the canoe." She says this with a half-smile, revealing gaps where teeth once were, knowing what I do not want to hear. I plead again, and she offers a maybe, though mostly to silence me. Sometimes plans lead to false, unpredictable capes, sometimes to a safe island haven. Sometimes "maybe" means yes.

tree house

MOST OF THE GROUNDS on our lot have been explored, corner to corner, compost pile to fire pit, front yard and back. Time to go up. We're going vertical, building a tree house, a skyward play space, an aerial porch.

Our project began with a trip to the library. We checked out *Tree-houses: The Art and Craft of Living Out on a Limb*. The cover shows a well-lit, watertight log structure high in some maples. Inside, Peter Nelson describes constructing a circular building that surrounds a 150-foot fir in British Columbia, propped up on six-by-eight beams fitted into custom metal brackets. While the book presents gorgeous photographs and drawings of tree houses from around the world, I was intimidated. I wanted to build a tree house, not a second home.

More to my tastes is *The Tree House Book* by David Stiles, geared for kids of all ages, with easier-to-follow instructions and illustrations: "The tree houses shown in this book are purposely made simple so a child could build them." Not so fast.

The first step in the construction of any arboreal habitat is site selection. We considered the empty lot down the street that we pass on the walk to school. It has a maple with low branches as well as a good sycamore with two trunks, but did we want the unknown intruder? At the corner of Eighth Street, we also pass the remains of a former loft wedged into maple branches, the tree beginning to heal over where lumber meets bark.

The woods down the street? We've seen remains of tree houses there too, with the cleated steps Stiles warns against: two-by-fours simply nailed into a tree can pull out and be dangerous. But the city owns the woods, and a citizens group manages it as a natural park. We could build one high up on the hill where no one would discover it, but tree houses rarely blend with their hosts, their straight geometry contrasting with the tree's wavy limbs. Besides, a maven of this group once scolded my daughter for scratching a rock outcropping. I'm all for natural preserves as sites for perpetuating biological diversity, but I'm with naturalist Robert Michael Pyle on this one: "For special places to work their magic on kids, they need to be able to do some clamber and damage. They need to be free to climb trees."

With that opportunity unavailable in our nearby woods, we chose the white pine straddled by hemlocks in our own yard. All three trees have had their trunks trimmed of low-lying branches, so access was good. The next decision was where in the tree. My son wanted it about twenty feet high in the crook where the main trunk splits off into four smaller vertical trunks. But when I went up there to inspect, twenty-three knee-wobbling ladder steps, I knew it was too high to be comfortable for both the builder and the dwellers. A good tree house should be high enough to feel euphoric but close enough to the ground to feel safe.

One approach to begin building would have been to carry some boards up and start nailing, but we tried to come up with a plan. I asked them to imagine a box up there and what branches might hold it up. Tree houses do nothing if not stir the imagination. Some of our favorite books are the Magic Tree House series, in which Jack and Annie can point to a book and say "I want to go there," and they do. From their leafy loft they travel to historical sites, Pompeii or medieval England, or natural ones, the Arctic or the desert, always on some mission, always aided by books. Elliot wanted a basket attached to a pulley for raising and lowering her kitten. Sam wanted a rope ladder like the illustration in the books. Neither thought much about how it would attach to the tree.

After some design hints from Stiles, we needed some wood. Harry Groot runs Next Generation Woods. He harvests wood in a sustainable, environmentally sound fashion and hangs a rough-sawn board in his shed etched with these words: "We do not inherit the earth from our ancestors—we borrow it from our children." While the kids petted the young goats (the kids), Groot and I loaded some stout poplar boards, true two-by-sixes, actually two inches by six inches, not the "dressed" lumber you buy at the big box. Groot and his wife, Gail, grow fine pasture-raised, Bourbon Red heritage turkeys too.

I used the eight-foot poplar boards to make the platform, the important part of any endeavor on which all else rests. I leveled two parallel to each other, hugging the tree (tree huggers) with six-inch lag bolts, and then put two more on top of those but perpendicular, the result like a game board for tic-tac-toe, a tree through the center square. I nailed more poplar two-by-sixes at right angles to these boards, and two more at each end to make a square frame, the last two resting out on the tips of the first two bottom joists—my favorite kind of work.

Operating on the principle that no kid will play in a tree house he or she has not had a hand in building, I sought their help for the rest. I thought a tree house, in addition to providing a platform for play, would give us something to do together on summer afternoons. It might also provide some benefits of learning, like how many inches in a foot, how many degrees in a right angle, and how to measure, saw, plane, hammer, and use a level. Sam sawed one end of our corner braces at my forty-five-degree mark, holding the saw with two hands, grunting and panting, while I worked on the notch at the other end, cutting off the corners to make a lip. Elliot helped toe-nail the bottom of the brace into the tree while Sam and I held it in place. She met resistance—the nail not going in very fast or bending, the hammer missing its target—but, tongue out to concentrate, like her dad, eventually it went in. Yes.

We worked this way for as long as I could keep their interest, or until other things did. We heard the mechanic whir of the cicadas while we worked, but then saw one emerging from its shell. At 10:00 its large, alien eyes—bug eyes—peered out. Lag bolts went into the first supports. By 10:30 it had fully shed its shell and climbed out on the tree. Holes drilled in another two-by-six cross member. By 11:30 it had unrolled its wings, letting them dry. We rode our bikes down to the grocery store for tuna fish and limeade. After lunch, the foundation was set. The cicada had taken flight.

We continued for several days, me giving the crew smaller tasks, like building furniture for their tree house, but they build it small, petite enough for the nearby squirrels, their nest in the next tree over, decorated with some ribbon the kids left in the lawn. We got sticky with pine sap, matting the hair on my legs, knotting that on

Elliot's head. A little cooking oil will take it off the hands, and rubbing alcohol is a good solvent for the hair.

"What are you building?" asks a curious neighbor when we meet on the sidewalk.

"A tree hut," I tell him. "For the kids," I have to add.

"What's in your tree?" another one asks, about the new view from the back alley. It seems the project is the talk of the town.

During another break, a friend arranges a visit for some neighborhood kids at the home of her boss, the area's richest man, rich enough to have his own aviary. In this he participates in a long line of falconry dating back to medieval kings. The caretaker, Bill, shows us an eagle owl, a northern goshawk, and some Harris hawks. Harris hawks, we learn, will hunt cooperatively. They hunt not only on sight, like goshawks, but on awareness of what other members in their group are doing: "I'll flush this rabbit from the thicket while you others ambush it," a strategy the kids employ to catch the new kitten. Crows, the intelligentsia of the avian world, can use tools. Evolutionary biologists think that cooperative hunting, the use of tools, and social behavior were key characteristics in the development of the mind.

I doubt building this tree house brought us leaps in intelligence, but I do know that kids their age learn best kinesthetically, by doing. Nail and saw, not watch and learn. Once the floor was on, more poplar, I put up four-by-four posts and a railing to secure them. I covered this bottom section with bark and wastewood slabs leftover from Harry's mill. It comes, as does much of Harry's wood, with pale-green lichen, blending in with the existing tree bark.

The kids helped me with this part. I handed them bark from the ladder below. They stood on the deck and leaned over the railing, two fledglings in their nest, papa bird feeding them nails. At a break, we took a bike ride down the New River Trail and scared up two bald eagles at river's edge, their remarkable comeback new to this area. One had a good-sized fish in its mouth; the other squawked at our intrusion. A bald eagle nest can be up to eight feet wide, the dimension of our new assemblage of sticks in a tree.

In *Children's Special Places*, David Sobel writes that in middle childhood "children feel a deep urge to move into the larger world away from home to find a place for themselves." And in finding a place for themselves, they are, in a sense, finding themselves. As we bond with our parents in early childhood, we bond with places between six and twelve, maintaining old relationships but creating new, no less significant ones. We start with small, temporary structures, bush houses, moving out to more larger, more permanent ones, the tree house, the neighborhood, the region, the world.

My own forts fit the pattern: with a friend I created one in the gully near the cemetery. We poured out our names from a box of powdered milk someone had dumped there, washed away by the next rain. We had one in the pine trees behind his house, one in the nearby small barn left abandoned, and finally one in the attic near the eyebrow window. We hardly used any of them, but using them is not the point. Building them is.

My children have created hideaways in the hemlocks and dens in the bamboo. Once my son and his friend dragged over the lumber and cabinetry from a nearby remodel, and they fit it together to form cubbies, created from hard materials but with flexible imaginations. They had walls around it and a flag pole, some spiky cones from a sweet gum tree stored in cinder blocks to throw at invading hordes. Elliot has built many-roomed forts from leaves: "If you guys are mean to me, that's where I'll go." They are fortlike in the way they provide shelter, but also in the way they fortify kids, provide nourishing retreats from the world. Creating a small, special place of their own is a small step toward becoming their own person.

With a few friends, Sam has one in a closet cove in his room. The sloping roof cuts off its height, making it tough for adults to fit in there, and a small, paneled door leads in, as through Alice's keyhole. They have written their names on the wall, to say "this is our territory," and they call themselves the "Green Apple Gang" because they like green apples. The password to enter is a secret. Kids' special places always are.

I see some small differences between genders, but not that much. My childhood buddy and I used to build snow fortifications for snowball fights. My sisters would build igloos and crawl inside. A friend and his sister used to argue about whose special place the creek was. He wanted a rock wall. She wanted a sitting room with chairs. Both my kids like to build terrariums for their plastic animals and Tupperware habitats for aquatic species soaked with clippings and rocks. They both like to make forts with the couch cushions and bedsheets, soft light filtered through the fabric. In *Speak, Memory*, Vladimir Nabokov recalls the cave behind the divan, "creeping through that pitch-dark tunnel," listening to the "singing in my ears." He also remembers the sensation of a "faint light that seemed to penetrate my penumbral covert" of a sheet tent, light from where "animals roamed in a landscape of lakes." Behind that linen veil, differences always seem less striking, difficulties more bearable.

That's one reason we're up in a tree, for protection. On some ancestral savanna, trees must have represented safety, a place to catch one's breath after acting on some flight response. One well-known Swiss family built a tree house "safe up there from jackals' visits during the night." But while protection might be one factor, a tree house for kids is mostly a new world, a place apart. When kids create these shelters, they discover these worlds, live on islands far from home, like another Robinson.

I stopped getting much help when it was time for the roof rafters and lath. So I climbed up the ladder myself, through pine boughs seeming to fight back by clutching my tool belt—"Oh no you don't"—nailing on rough-cut cedar shingles: scent of pine joined with aromatic cedar. From the ground, the hip roof (as in four-corner pyramid shaped, not as in cool, suave roof) is most conspicuous, the orange cedar not yet faded and mossy. It has holes cut in it for the upper boughs to poke through, which drape the sides of the hut in pine needles and cones. The whole thing looks suspended in evergreen clouds. Up close the bark of the tree is crenulated and gray, the color of a great horned owl or our bushy-tailed neighbors, or they are the color of it.

The rhythm on the metal roof outside my office window reports the movement of these squirrels. They are busy burying food caches for winter, energy for a later time. The nuts they hoard in the grass may be eaten in late fall or early winter, but they may also be left to grow into a sapling some spring.

In many ways a tree house or any special place kids build is merely a dress rehearsal for their eventual departure, for when they will ultimately leave this nest. "I love the new tree house," my daughter tells me as she begins to put some of her things up there, making it her own. "A high up in the leafy branches / Cozy as can be house," poet Shel Silverstein writes, capturing what is doubly exciting about a tree house, "free house," "A secret you and me house": both its height and its sense of security.

We invited the neighbors to a tree house party, "a party in a tree," so said our invites. The kids climbed up and down all evening. The next morning, I found their food stores left up there. One attendee has since reported back: they're building a tree house in their neighbor's oak. It's going to be bigger than ours, and higher. "And it's going to have a rope ladder," she adds, so there.

On the last night of summer we built a fire in the backyard with the excess scraps of wood. Afterward, we brought the sleeping bags up to the tree house. Sam and Elliot slept alone up there. Before I turned in I went out to check on them, could hear their hushed voices over the chirr of field crickets. No electricity, no video game, just rock and sway in the needled wind. Up there, happy endings are attainable. Love is secure—it is bolted to a tree.

seven days

WHAT DO YOU DO when your seven-year-old son tells you he wants to take a seven-day trip? I think he got the idea by reading about buckskin explorers such as Lewis and Clark, but he had it fixed in his mind that we would go, for seven days, me and him, outside. We would fish and hike and camp, like they did a long time ago.

He told his friends and his teacher, and when it came time to draw a picture of what he would do that summer, he filled his with animals and wrote: "I am going on a seven day chrip." He was going into second grade then. Now he is in third. We have a picture frame that holds photographs of each grade. Each year of school might as well be a geologic epoch, secondary to tertiary, so much changes in kids.

On a wooden, swinging door in the kitchen we also keep a height scale in pencil. Each birthday and on random days in between, we line them up, backs straight, feet on the floor, and use a cereal box to help mark off how tall they have grown. On the back of that wall we have a thin map of the Appalachian Trail. In my mind I sometimes merge the two, trail and chart, so that I measure off their growth by distance on the map. Up at the top, when they are full grown, Mount Katahdin. About now, Delaware Water Gap.

So that's what we decided we would do: fish a little and hike some on the AT down near Mount Rogers, the highest mountain in Virginia, formerly Balsam Mountain. We made lists and packed our gear. On Route 16, the sign outside the Sugar Grove Baptist Church quoted from Proverbs: "And he that begetteth a wise child shall have joy of him."

The first two days we fished, first at a nearby stocked lake and then a wild stream. Then we left the campground for the mountains. The trail switched back sharply up Beech Mountain, 3,550 feet. On the way up, it soon became clear that we had different ideas about the day's schedule. He stopped for every potential salamander spot and for all millipede and spider crossings, a screeching halt, no easy feat with a thirty-pound pack on. Sam had fully intended to carry much of his own gear, but he began shedding stuff from his pack early. I took his sleeping bag and most of his clothes. He kept his wooden gun and the canteen he insisted on.

Then to Buzzard Rock, on the southern slope of Whitetop, the second highest mountain in Virginia. Finally, we walked around Whitetop Mountain itself and down to Elk Garden, where we made camp in the woods next to a large boulder. Sam was glad to be through with the day's hiking and to have some time to himself, lying fallow, downtime. He climbed the boulder and scouted the woods, brought back some sticks for a fire and located the spring. So we divided our labor. He took care of fire and water. I was in charge of food and shelter—dried food, that is, and a small tent. Saving time.

At home, there would be homework to do and dinner to make

and the phone to answer. I might have to shuttle the kids to dance or soccer. Then there's that thirty-five hours per week most American kids need with the *screen*—something that shelters or shields us from the outside world. Days and weeks blitz by in a fast-forward blur. No time to wander through the woods or pick through leaves. Time out. Free time.

At night, we read from an "illustrated classic" version of *Robinson Crusoe*, who scored time on a post: "Every seventh day he cut a notch through the six notches, and so marked off a week." The seven-day week comes to us from the astrologers of Babylon, about 2,700 years ago. The time in between moons became a *moonth*, now month. Because about seven days elapsed between each phase of the moon, the Babylonian calendar showed four periods of seven days. They based the week, from a German word for "turn" or "change," on the seven known "planets" or luminaries, including the sun and moon, each with its own deity, each twenty-four hours divine.

In the morning, we hiked on through Deep Gap to a little spur that took us to Mount Rogers itself, 5,729 feet. We took breaks every hour, with stoppages in between. We ate lunch in a spruce grove with wood shavings on the ground, savoring peanut butter and honey on bread smooshed in the pack. We took a long break there, making castles with the wood shavings, adding more with a pen knife.

Then to the peak itself, but the top of Rogers is more a rounded hump enclosed by Fraser firs, slowly dying from a pest. As summits go, it is not an impressive one, no breathtaking view. The only way we knew we topped out was the brass U.S. Geological Survey benchmark placed in the rock, which allowed more time to sit.

* * *

For adults, time fades, washes out our brights, wears away our denim (shrinks it some too), though we barely notice it happening—maybe the very wear and tear itself prevents us. For our own lives, there is no clear summit from which to view events, no trail guide to chart our progress because it has slowed to a crawl. But we do notice the milestones of kids, because they happen so often. First word. First steps. Fit in a carrier on your back one year, climb up the tallest mountain the next.

Spend time with your children and experiences intensify, take on a special poignancy. Watching Sam come up the mossy trail and in the cool, thin air, I had the odd sensation that I was watching myself outside myself. Not too much is new as we grow older, but with children we rediscover the newness and brightness we once knew, the potential in a pile of wood shavings. Blink and they will pass you by—reach summits before you do.

On the first day of summer, longest day of the year, the earth tilting back toward darkness, we needed another layer as we descended and washed our faces in the clouds. We warmed up and rested at Thomas Knob shelter. I scribbled in my notebook, and Sam drew a picture of a boy with his tongue hanging out.

* * *

At seven a young person understands little about time and the passing of it. They still live close to the present, looking more toward the near future. Every moment is a now, and days are a stream of them we can never step in twice. The *nows* slip *past*, the *future* becomes *present*. On this trip I realized we could come back and do this hike again, but it wouldn't be the same. His legs would never be that skinny or his two little feet that small. He would never ask the same questions: How did they used to make fish hooks? All the hikes from here on out are mostly one way. We get to walk the same trails, but not the same steps. Since we never return it, we do not borrow time but have to steal it, snatch it from whatever takes time.

Reflect too much on the changes in children and the slipping of time, and you find yourself sitting on the sidelines, sulking on the bench. But some sense of the transience of time is also necessary for the liberation from it, for the recognition that all was made a long time ago—250 million years ago in the case of these Appalachian Mountains—and you were born for this.

We reached Rhododendron Gap at the right time, when the tunnels of waxy laurels were peaking pink. The ancient Greeks distinguished between two kinds of time, *chronos* and *kairos*. While the former refers to chronological or sequential time, the latter signifies "a time in between," a right or opportune moment. *Chronos* can be measured with clocks, while *kairos*, if measured at all, is located in moments and events, is spiral and organic, an "inner cadence that brings fruit to ripeness," blossoms to color.

Then on through Fat Man Squeeze, where the trail shimmies through rock, and along Wilburn Ridge, with magnificent views of the valleys and ridges below and their folds like rumpled bedclothes. Finally, we arrived in Grayson Highlands, still in the Crest Zone, rugged and rocky, a windswept meadow created through logging and fire but kept bald by free-roaming ponies. My wife and daughter met us for the last half mile, ran into us up on that high plain. They, horse lovers, skipped with the ponies and we, weary feet, ground down to the car. Seven years ago on a hiking trip in the Cascades, on our honeymoon, my pregnant wife experienced some cramps and spotting. We weren't sure if Sam would be here. Gestation time.

* * *

The Greeks had another word, *ekstasis*, meaning "outside standing," or "standing outside oneself." Environmental psychologist Louise Chawla has located these moments in autobiographies, *kairotic* moments of unmediated contact with the world. Chawla says they "shine like jewels within the casing of our lives," giving us "meaningful images; an internalized core of calm; and a sense of integration with nature." They are sweet spots in time.

The next day we fished some more and then headed home. I don't remember why. Did we run out of food? Were we too tired? We hiked 6.9 miles the third day and 7.1 the fourth, but we lasted only five total days. Sam was disappointed in our leaving, but he was also looking forward to getting home. "Next time, Dad, *seven days*," but we have yet to make it back. But he remembers the trip, remembers our lunch in the spruce grove and the pink Catawba buds, the squeeze through the rock and the ponies grazing. I don't know yet if the trip will shine like a jewel, or give him some reservoir of strength late in life, but we will try again next turn of the earth. Next time.

tide pools

CONSIDER THE LIFE of an ordinary shell. It harbors and protects a soft body within. It may come in different shapes and sizes, cone or conch, scallop or clam. It may be discarded, washed up on shore, ground down into sand unless recycled, when a new life may move in, may itself move on like a hermit crab.

Consider a car. It houses tender bodies that will cram the available space within, taking on the shape as their own. After long periods of time, it may also seem too small, other life forms taking over, becoming smelly, as when shells and crab carapaces are left in it for too long. Eventually, it will deposit its inhabitants on some far shore.

At the beginning of the summer the kids said they wanted to visit the coast and learn something about tide pools. The best time to engage children is during that high tide when they are motivated, but summer came and went, and we did not make it to the coast. Seems they had some memory of time spent at the Jersey shore when they were younger, catching crabs and playing in a little pool left behind as the ocean receded, where they found shark teeth and shells—smooth blue inside, all spikes and spirals out.

So it was necessary to make one more trip, but real tide pools are found on the rocky coast, some eight hundred miles away in Maine. More a pilgrimage really, since part of the purpose for the trip lay in the fact that Rachel Carson—whose 1956 essay, "Help Your Child to Wonder," has been an inspiration to this book—spent summers on the coast near the town of Boothbay Harbor.

Carson had an endless fascination with the life that inhabited the low-tide holes on the rocky shores of Maine. Tide pools, she thought, mirrored the "spectacle of life in all its varied manifestations as it has appeared, evolved, and sometimes died out." In rocky basins at the threshold of the sea, she wrote, in *The Edge of the Sea*, "the drama of life played its first scene on earth and perhaps even its prelude."

Though Carson grew up miles inland near Pittsburgh, the lure of the sea led to training as an aquatic biologist, a job with the U.S. Fish and Wildlife Service, and three books: *Under the Sea Wind* (1941), *The Sea Around Us* (1951), and *The Edge of the Sea* (1955). In her third book Carson explores three different shorelines—rock, sand, and coral—and describes how life is shaped by the tides, temperature, geology, the force of the surf, and currents of the sea, especially the communities that thrive between the tide lines.

She peered into the narrow crevices and deep fissures of the rugged Maine coast and saw both the frailty and insistence with which creatures, battered by waves and weather, held on for life. And after discovering endless mysteries between the tides and the interconnectedness of all life, Carson took action. Her fourth book was a distress call, a mayday about the dangers to human and biological health caused by pesticides. Linda Lear, her biographer, writes that "she could not stand idly by and say nothing when all that was in jeopardy, when human existence itself was endangered." *Silent Spring* (1962) was a singular act of courage, for Carson took on the chemical companies and the government agencies in describing the toxic effects of pesticides and the lives they harmed, even as she herself was dying of cancer.

Before time ran out, Carson had fully intended to expand the essay she published in *Woman's Home Companion* and turn it into a book. She told her agent, Marie Rodell, that the material "comes to my door without half trying." But as cancer and a "catalogue of illnesses" advanced, writing became a physical impossibility. On November 3, 1963, she wrote to her friend Dorothy Freeman that "there is still so much I want to *do*, and it is hard to accept that in all probability, I must leave most of it undone." "There are times," she anguished, "when I get so tired of the pain and especially the crippling that if it were not for those I love most, I'd want it to end soon." But then she adds, "I want very much to do the Wonder book. That would be Heaven to achieve."

* * *

Before we arrived in Maine, we stopped in New Haven and the Beinecke Rare Book and Manuscript Library, home of a Gutenberg Bible, a sunken sculpture garden, translucent marble panes, and Carson's papers.

Carson wrote to Marie Rodell on January 22, 1959, about a possible table of contents for an expansion of "Help Your Child to Wonder," but earlier, undated notes fill in the outline. The book would have ten chapters, one on "The Sky," "The Sea" (of course), and "The Woods."

Indented underneath, with space for more, she wrote "old stumps, lichens, birds."

She would have four chapters on "The Changing Year," a chapter for each season. On a page with the words "Winter" centered at the top, she wrote "theme: life dormant but waiting," and she wanted to capture how "tracks in snow reveal life which there may be no evidence of." In that chapter she wanted to capture "crystals, blue shadows, what finds shelter, the beauty of trees without leaves." In a box in the lower right-hand corner, she made a list of possible sources: "Field Book of Animals in Winter, Audubon leaflet, Thoreau."

She had planned to do a chapter on the "The World of Tiny Things," which she also called "Worlds Within Worlds." On a separate page, she wrote "Specific incidents: listening for veeries, Rock Creek, first starfish, first urchin, ghost crabs, surf, wind, walk in rainy woods" and "Southport," her summer home. Underneath, she wrote "foxes and deer, reindeer moss."

That would lead to "The Miracle of Life": "cocoons, leaf buds, tadpoles, plant seeds." On this topic, she wanted to capture the "reverence for life," the word *reverence* underlined, "no thoughtless or unnecessary killing."

At the top of other pages, she made notes of material that would go in the original essay, later published with photographs by Charles Pratt and titled *The Sense of Wonder* (1965). She begins that piece by telling how she wrapped her young nephew Roger in a blanket on a stormy night and brought him down to the sea edge. A few nights later, they went out with a flashlight, searching for ghost crabs, "sand-colored, fleet-legged beings." In *The Edge of the Sea*, she thought a small crab "alone with the sea" could be a symbol for life itself: "for the delicate, destructible, yet incredibly vital force that somehow holds its place amid the harsh realities of the inorganic world." In *The Sense of Wonder*, she wrote that the "sight of these small living creatures, solitary and fragile against the brute force of the sea, had moving philosophic overtones," but she did not pretend that she and Roger "reacted with similar emotions."

In her notes, Carson simply wrote "The World of Night," "ghost crabs, katydids, migratory birds," and "moonlight over water." Under "The World of Sound," she wrote "wind, thunder, surf—the great sounds of nature." She also noted "Bird chorus at dawn," which, she explained in the final piece, "no child should be unaware of," and then she etched the words "exploring with a flashlight." In *The Sense of Wonder*, she promises Roger that they will explore the garden insects at night, the "insect orchestra," and she tells of one "fairy bell ringer." In an unpublished piece called "October Night," she describes it this way:

> Your brain may tell you that you are listening to the stridulations
> of the snowy tree cricket, but though you try to be ever so matter
> of fact, you will be able to think of nothing but fairies when you
> hear it. It is exactly the sound that should come from a bell held in
> the hand of the tiniest elf—inexpressibly clear and silvery, so faint,
> so barely-to-be-heard, so ghostly, that you hold your breath as
> you bend closer to the green glades from which the fairy chiming
> comes.

On another of her notebook pages, she jotted down that "the twittering voices of birds lead to the mystery of migration" and "birds across moon," both of which received attention in the final piece, but she also listed "spring peepers, whippoorwill, nighthawk, owl," which did not.

Under "Sound of Wind": "in forest, blowing around house, chorus of many voices." "A child in bed in a storm can be told names [underlined] of the great winds of the world and to imagine places they blow." "Effect on people," she scribbled, "mistral," and then something that looks like "willy wow," and something that looks like "roaring 40s."

"Nature Isn't All Fair Weather" headlined another page, though the topics were clearly overlapping by now: "the woods in the rain, the stormy beach," both with check marks next to them, as if they had already been covered.

"What if you had never seen it before?" she asked at the top of the next, a question that made it into the final piece. Underneath, she marked "the stars on Dogfish Head," an incident she describes in the published version, but also "sunrise, moonlight on rocks, stars in the rocks," starfish that must mirror the sky.

On the next page, she asked, "Who, once aware of the mystery of rain, could ever again be untouched by a sense of wonder as it splashes in his face?" Rain must have reminded her of smell, because on the next page she wrote "The World of Scent," which would include "the sharp, good smell of wood smoke rising from a chimney" and the many separate odors of low tide, both of which received passing mention. "Sun on spruce, fir, juniper, apples in sun," though savored often, she had yet to pay tribute to.

"The Best Things Are Free," Carson titled the next page, but no more. "Don't Take It for Granted," she scrawled on the next. Nothing more about that either.

She wanted to get to the "Before" and "After" of what we see. "Rain, the water cycle, shore birds, purple sandpipers running over reef when R [Roger] is older, will begin to tell him of journey from Arctic. Sand. Grain."

Her own sense of wonder is clearly revealed in this outline haiku, and Carson strongly believed that you had to cultivate wonder as a foundation to facts. "Awe and wonder are stimulated by knowledge in the adult. The more we learn, the more wonder grows," she jotted in her notes. "But in children, cultivate the wonder as a foundation for facts." An important theme to "the Wonder book" would be this direct pathway into the unity and awe of nature:

It is important for a child to have some direct knowledge, from an early age, of lives other than human—some of the thousands upon thousands of species that, even as he does, inhabit this earth. He should be aware of them, not as creatures described in books, or as a word in a crossword puzzle, but animals living in his own world, searching for food, caring for their young, struggling to survive in the face of difficulties.

"To understand the shore," begins the preface to *The Edge of the Sea*, "it is not enough to catalogue its life." Instead, we must sense the "long rhythms of earth and sea that sculptured its land forms" and feel "the surge of life beating always at its shores—blindly, inexorably pressing for a foothold." It was not enough to pick up a shell and say "this is a murex" or "that is an angel wing." Carson would have us intuit "the whole life of the creature that once inhabited this empty shell: how it survived amid surf and storms, what were its enemies, how it found food and reproduced."

* * *

She underlined "Concepts" and, underneath, "sense of removal of seasons." "Nature," she also penned in her notes, "the greatest tranquilizer of all. Walk in woods or field the best relief for tension." Finally, she addressed the central question of *The Sense of Wonder:* "Is exploring the natural world just a pleasurable way to pass the golden hours of childhood or is there something deeper? I am sure there is something much deeper—the development of an inner resource of strength that will endure as long as a man or woman lives."

And then she added, "Albert Einstein expressed it when he said the most beautiful and most profound emotion we can experience is the sense of the mystical. He to whom this emotion is a stranger, who can no longer wonder and stand rapt in awe, is as good as dead." But, perhaps recognizing a sentiment too strong for a popular magazine of the time, she crossed this out.

The final chapter, the capstone of the book, would be called "The Beauty in Nature." She wrote to Marie Rodell that "obviously, there could be possible overlapping. For example, "the Cocoon to Butterfly series could go into Chapter 4 (The Changing Year: Spring) or 9 (The Miracle of Life)." The last chapter, she wrote to Rodell, would "provide a place for beautiful scenes as well as for beauty in a smaller and more intimate concept," but clearly beauty intersected with much of what she would have already written.

Woods, sky, and sea were all beautiful to her, children themselves, part of the nature they observe, things of beauty. In "The World of Tiny Things," she might have covered her beloved tide pools, if she didn't already touch on them in the chapter on the sea. And in "The Miracle of Life," she would have to write of the beauty of birth. This would include a story of her nephew Roger, small enough to call blackbirds "croads," watching a mother feed its babies. "I can't," she wrote, "pretend to know what went on in the mind behind the baby eyes that watched this but," and then her handwriting ends, no ellipsis. But what?

Since knowledge for Carson was so often secondary to wonder, it almost seems her own reverence rendered her speechless. Clearly, she wanted to remind us of a fundamental truth easy to forget: that children recognize the beauty and unity of the world they are a part of though they may hardly be conscious of it. They are shielded from the world of philosophizing by their very intimacy with their environment, free to delicately watch tiny miracles of life unfold.

* * *

Under a full, harvest moon, we arrived late in Boothbay Harbor but with some time to walk around the water's edge. We peered into the inlet and saw flashes of minnows, long strings of dark kelp, and flecks of shells reflected in the harbor lights and moon. The kids kept spying moving things, crabs coming out to survey and then ducking back in under rocky cover. We saw two submerged ones ambling toward each other to fight or mate or possibly both. My family was anticipating what we would see the next day, and maybe forgiving me for bringing them on this long odyssey.

In the morning, we went to Ocean Point, where Carson liked to go tide pooling. We caught the flood tide, the water world returning to shore. Sam and Elliot jumped from rock to rock and picked up shells in between. We found a few tide pools, mostly high ones with scarce life accustomed to a prolonged absence of the sea. In them some small, barely visible forms moved. "Lilliputian beings," Carson called them, "swimming through dark pools that lie between the grains of sand." Under the blue sky we saw lichens pale green and bright orange and collected relics of crabs, sea urchins, and star fish. We rescued one crab washed into a tight crack and dying of exposure, barely able to close his claw until reunited with the restorative sea. Sam found one hole he thought was decorated with foliage like some great hall for welcoming fish. "You can write about this in your book." Elliot draped kelp around her neck like a fashionable mink, then on her head like a sea goddess, a kelp woman.

In the afternoon we walked through the woods of a nearby island, through tall spruces and some dwarf, with a spongy layer of pine duff and lichen underneath our feet. We took off our shoes and walked on the lichen carpet, "reindeer moss" it is called because it looks like antlers. For Carson, "they have the quality of fairyland," as did so much of the natural world she peered closely into. Keyholes took us out to the coast, with views of nearby islands and the water's edge, fragrance of pine mixed with seacoast, elemental earth and water.

Then in the afternoon, just before low tide, we walked out over ground that was underwater in the morning, over the slippery rocks, every space and gap covered in slick seaweed. The only good foothold was on the millions of sharp, exposed barnacles. In the clear pools themselves, green waves of seaweed rolled in and back out with the ocean. There were spidery tubes, wide noodles, hairy fibers, and something like brown parsley. We saw the small periwinkle shells first, then mussels and a sea urchin, and suddenly, as the tide receded more and more, the stars came out. It was as if our eyes became accustomed to the shape, and then they were everywhere: green ones and pink ones and some navy blue. "Here, I found one. It's pink, over here," shouted Elliot, holding a star in her palm. "I have some too," said Sam. "Lots of them!" There were creatures so exquisite, so colorful and oddly formed they seemed almost unreal, but each stalk and tentacle has its place and function, waiting for the incoming force, sweeping the water for all it needs to live.

Finally, when the tide was at its lowest, we came to a cave. In the first few pages of *The Edge of the Sea*, Carson describes a "fairy cave," a place that for her stood apart for "its revelation of exquisite beauty" and its "fairy pool." She knelt on a "wet carpet of sea moss and looked back into the dark cavern that held the pool in a shallow basin." In that pool, "a mirror had been created in which all that grew on the ceiling was reflected in the still water below."

When we looked into our cave, a tide pool below us and wet dripping roof above, swells coming occasionally close, it too felt otherworldly, like we were suspended on some elusive intertidal boundary, granted a momentary glimpse into the threshold of the sea.

In *The Sense of Wonder*, Carson describes how Roger learned the shells on her rocky Maine coast, known to him as "winkies" (periwinkles), "weks" (whelks), and "mukkies" (mussels). She wanted Roger to enjoy things parents might otherwise deny children because of inconvenience: wet shoes or clothes, dirt that must be cleaned off the floor, or staying out past bedtime.

> We have let him join us in the dark living room before the big picture window to watch the full moon riding lower and lower toward the far shore of the bay, setting all the water ablaze with silver flames and finding a thousand diamonds in the rocks on the shore as the light strikes the flakes of mica embedded in them.

Carson hoped that the memory of that scene, repeated year after year, tide after rising tide, would "mean more to him in manhood than the sleep he was losing." "He told me it would, in his own way," sitting quietly on his Aunt Rachel's lap. "Watching the moon and the water and all the night sky," he whispered the words, "I am glad we came."

On a long trip like the one we took, like any trip with children, we drift between the sublime treasures revealed at some far shore and the near debris of plastic toys and used crayons washed up in the car. We ate bad road food and some great, once we arrived in Maine (steamahs and lobstahs), fought bronchial infections, lack of sleep, closed motels, and achy backs. But was it worth it? Was it worth it to walk in Carson's footsteps, among her fairy sprites, picking up shells and peering into the world of tiny things while the tides surged like the whole Atlantic coast breathing, if just for a little while? I won't pretend to know what went on in the minds behind my children's eyes, but—looking out that big picture window—I am glad we went.

dirt world

ONE EASY STEP toward getting kids out the door is to *keep shoes close*. My kids are old enough now to go out on their own, but if they can't find their shoes, they might not go. In fact, if anything distracts them when we are making our way out, the moment may have passed. One solution here is to emphasize that they don't need shoes. Though I'm a hopeless tenderfoot, I still love the feel of grass under my feet. But if it's cold out, we've solved the problem of keeping shoes handy by building a shoe shelf near the door. When we lived in Slovenia, we became accustomed to slipping shoes off when we came inside. Slovenians always have some kind of rack for holding outdoor shoes and indoor slippers, and now we have one too. We also keep rain and snow boots in a bench on the porch. Making it easy to slip on the shoes makes it easy to slip out the door.

There are other things to keep close as well, like the jackets and gloves. We keep our tents and sleeping bags in a chest on the porch, so that when it's time to go, it's easy to pack. And if the expedition will be long, say an hour or more, I must bring snacks and water. If they are enticing enough, these in themselves may get the kids out. When we have what we need, we must also gather the other items we may want to bring: field guides, a set of binoculars, and stuffed or plastic animal toys—characters in the play. The kids put these items in their backpacks, but I know I'll end up with them.

Another way to get kids outside is to make indoor items outdoor ones, to *take out the toys*. One November day I enticed the kids out by suggesting we take some of the stuffed animals for a boat ride. With boots on we trudged down to the creek and chased plastic containers and their contents floating and bobbing down the mini-rapids. We have also raced trucks down the hill, crashing them into the water. Sometimes they get lost on the way down, hung up in a downed log or lost in a leaf pile, and a search-and-rescue must ensue. My wife and her friends used to play plane wreck, actually scattering their toys and clothes in the woods and inventing scenarios for the survivors. A sandbox isn't that necessary. A pile of dirt will work just as well for making racetracks or a moated castle. Our friends have a dirt pile so special it has its own name, "dirt world." On a summer night, after tramping through a nearby meadow, the kids spent the rest of their time there, using it as the mother ship, and snaking toys through its gopher holes.

To encourage my children to roam in fields and the world out there, even one made of dirt (what our world is anyway), I want to *take down the fence*. When we moved into our new house, our first child, Sam, was very young. The yard had a fence on the sides and back and a hedge out front with two openings: one for the car and one to walk through. Both of these outlets led to the street, and though we live on a quiet one, we worried that Sam might wander out there, so we built gates. Now that my kids are older, they rove more freely, but they rarely leave the yard. Across the street is a church parking lot that is scooter- and bike-riding central to most neighborhood kids. And behind our alley is a great sledding hill only partly wooded. At one end our neighbors planted bamboo as a privacy break. The kids love to explore and hide in there, but they hardly ever venture farther.

The fence between our yard and the world beyond is metaphorical too. I fear that in emphasizing the danger of the road, we've limited their ability to seek and explore, to be curious about the world beyond the fence, so they hew close to the yard. But exploration comes at different stages of development: more recently they've begun to ride bikes around the block, and to ping-pong back and forth between each other's yards. Taking down the fence also means letting them get dirty and wet. The only way to experience the world around you is to jump right in.

Removing the fence relates to removing the fear. Another way to get kids outside is by helping them to *not be afraid of the dark*. Think of the freedom of playing outside when you were young. Remember those games of tag or home free or kickball lasting until dusk, until you heard it was "Time to come in now. It's getting dark." So what if it's getting dark? Each time we say it, we only reinforce the fear. From the lit inside, it may look dark out, but it's just the magical time when the lightning bugs come out, as do the stars.

We've tried to learn our nighttime sounds too, to tell the katydids from the crickets, the hoppers from the peepers. We also try our hand making owl calls, "who cooks for you all" (the barred owl), though my screech owl sounds too much like a horse's whinny. Catching moths is easy: just hang a white sheet outside a window where light radiates, and watch them gather. To attract sugaring moths, mix a concoction of beer, sugar, molasses, a very ripe banana, some fruit juice if you have it, and a shot of rum. After letting it stew for a day or so, paint it on fence posts or trees in late summer. When it works, the moths jostle for space on the sweet patch. If it doesn't, you'll still have butterflies and other insects the next day.

Nighttime generates its excitement, but also its own calm. The best thing to do at night is celebrate it with a backyard fire. Forget the marshmallows. Just sit down on the grass and welcome the dusking blue-black. Nearly all cultures celebrate the change of seasons with some kind of festival of light. Easter comes in spring, when children traditionally danced around the maypole and villages lit fires on the hillsides. The ancient Celts and Saxons celebrated May First as Beltane, or "the day of fire." Christmas comes at a time when pagans used to celebrate the solstice, when fires were lit to strengthen and welcome back the sun on its return to summer—a tradition carried forth in the Yule log.

When I pull down my beanstalks and pull up my tomato stakes, I know it is fall. My kids feel it too, in the cold mornings on our walks to school and in the smell of leaf mold. To get kids outside, *take back the seasons*. They should know fall by the signs of harvest, not the items on the store shelf. If our children are once again to be members of the landscapes they inhabit, they need to know where the sun sets, and when the berries ripen.

Last year, on "Black Friday," the busiest shopping day of the year, we walked on the New River Trail. As we drove home with our collections—interesting rocks, a turkey feather, the sightings of a great blue heron and a broad-winged hawk—we saw others returning from their gathering: bright red shopping bags and sparkling packages. Perhaps they stem from the same impulse. In autumn, some head to the woods, newly laid bare by fallen leaves, to explore their bare necessities, or they pick food in the fields. Still heeding an ancient call to hoard and gather against the oncoming winter, we can also head to the stores.

When they feel that urge to gather, I try to take them outside to do it: we *go fishing*. Every walk with children turns up some treasure to keep, and though we want to encourage them to "take only memories," sometimes a bird feather has to come along. But we fish for live things as well. Lakes and ponds are filled with obliging bluegills. They have prickly dorsal fins so we're careful when taking fish off the hook, but there is no easier fish to catch. Or we hunt for crayfish and salamanders, in the creek close by, or tadpoles in a nearby pond. Kids loves tadpoles, love the metamorphosis of butterflies too, as they are themselves changing, learning to walk on land and take flight. Fight those trips to the store by taking them out to gain some purchase on the world around them. Go out to get filled up.

Perhaps most importantly, if the kids are to get out, I will have to *find time*. We are usually in a rush to go somewhere, from one organized activity to another. I've heard many people describe their sense that time has picked up pace. Children used to have whole stretches of time to think and wander or pick through clover. "I used to spend hours in the backyard," writes Annie Dillard, "thinking God knows what, and peeling the mottled bark of a sycamore, idly, littering the grass with dried lappets and strips." Letting them off the achievement treadmill, ironically, leads to more creative, resilient kids.

They need the organized, linear play but also the creative, lateral kind. Let them move about and referee their own disputes. And get them out of that contraption that flattens landscape and compresses time. We used to set up Osage orange (a green gourd that we called brains) speed bumps to slow down the cars. Have them tromp around on foot or bike, listen to creaks and songbirds, taste the wind and morning mist, and take time to feel the old dirt world go round.

If it is important that kids get outside, *make your peace with the screen*. We've all seen that glazed-over look kids get when watching a show, or their mouths drooling over the game pad. I know one family that requires half an hour of exercise for every hour of TV time. Going outside leads to greater fulfillment than does learning about nature on a computer. Young, developing kids also learn kinesthetically, by movement, but too often they are stuffed in rows where they learn about nature rather than from it. And when they learn from it, they start to develop a reverence for it.

During a day off for Easter vacation, my wife and I left the kids home alone for a few hours in the afternoon (we were both within close reach by phone). When I came home, beautiful spring day, they were both holed up in front of their screen of choice. I suggested an alternative activity, that we pull the wagon down to a dry creekbed and pick out some rocks for a fire pit. They turned the rocks over, different shapes, sizes, colors, and textures.

"How big?"

"As big as your head."

"How's this one?"

"Is that your head?"

With another friend, they formed a chain gang to relay them up the bank. Then, like a bobsled team, we pushed our wheeled sled up the hill, taking turns as anchor person, side runners, and steerer: "keep it straight," "whoa, to the left." We negotiated flattest and smoothest ride home, taking breaks, working together to hoist it over curb cuts and across streets. We lifted, we pushed, we pulled and steered—we moved. We also took in the birdsong of a spring afternoon, saw a purple crocus shooting up through a fringe of brown leaves, and wondered at the fluorescent-green tassels hanging from trees—catkins, we later learned, waiting to be dispersed by the wind.

So many technologies are so seductive that refraining from using them can seem like fighting an addiction. We swore off video games in our house, but Sam encountered them at a neighbor's house and with his older cousins. He grew so fascinated with them (as children inevitably do with things off limits) that one day he cut out a TV screen from a cardboard box, drew controls on the bottom, and then made hand held remotes with the leftover scrap. He stared at his empty box, moving his imaginary joysticks, playing a game in his mind. Lest this sound like a good idea, it was somewhat pathetic to watch.

We stick to strict limits: no more than an hour every other day, after homework and chores, conditional upon a good report card and general good behavior. But sometimes I think that, left alone (in a state of nature, the philosophers used to say), he would play video games all the time. When we talked to him once about how we thought this new device in our house had too much power and priority over his life, he responded like a true addict: "I can control it." We made it through TV-Turnoff Week in April with no signs of withdrawal, no sweating or agitation. We did notice increased attention, better listening and interaction with one another, and a general sense that we weren't as pressed for time.

As I write this, I'm granted a little writing time because the kids are finishing a movie. If I want them to get out today, I may have to *be their guide*. We are in now, but later we will wash the dog and take a walk along the river.

Before I had kids, I was father to a dog. Mookie was an athletic lab mix known for wanting to get out and go with. He would stay alongside me, without a leash, barely containing his enthusiasm, but when he sensed the run, walk, or hike was on, indicated by your first step or wave of the hand, he shot out of a cannon, and was never happier. Even our new kitten gets us out, in ways. The other morning she chased the squirrels off the bird feeder and high up into the tulip poplar outside our bedroom window. With the aid of a tall ladder, I coaxed her down. Pets can bring the outside world in too, literally in the case of some cats who like to show off their catch or chase it through the house. But also in the ways they allow kids to interact with animals, learn what they respond to, and, by extension, how to care for other species and nature more broadly.

Dogs love to hike, and kids hike better both with a dog to chase and with other kids to keep up with, so sometimes it's useful to *organize a hike date*. We visit the wildflowers in spring and take trips through our park with local naturalists. No need for hiking boots or extensive gear—go on "sneaker hikes" that are more about play and being together than getting to the summit. Head for areas that offer more than the trail and a nice view. Kids like hikes along creeks or around ponds, where there is more likely to be wildlife.

When they come with those three words a parent hates to hear, "I am bored," tell them what your parents told you. Go outside. Go out the door and away from the all-too-comfortable. We know that it is an old folk belief that you get sick from the rain or cold. Keeping children inside, however, can actually make them sicker. One theory for why asthma is on the rise is that Americans spend an estimated 90 percent of their time indoors and have higher exposures to allergens.

Of course, parents could use some help. Developers, city councils, and planning commissions could help by not paving over or otherwise "improving" every square inch of available play and open space and by creating networks of trails and greenways, safe pathways that connect kids to one another and to nature. Schools and their governing boards could help by making outdoor learning more central to the curriculum, or perhaps by making outdoor play the afternoon's "homework." Learning the wildflowers in one's own landscape, or even the plants that live outside the classroom door, ranks much lower on the list of educational priorities than do abstract factoids about plant parts—to prepare for the siege of May testing. But learning to find wonder and beauty in the world kids will live in—learning self-reliance and about taking responsibility for the world they inhabit—ranks higher on most parental scales. After all, the ultimate goal of parenting is to help kids figure out what they can do with themselves on their own time, something only experience can teach, something spending time outside in nature knows best.

We belong out there. There's a rich, multifarious, lush green world outside that we are a part of. And it's healthy. Good for the body, and yes, good for the soul. "Outside lies magic," says John R. Stilgoe. Outside lies a world of marvels, a thousand dormant associations to be tucked away and recalled later in life. Outside lie stories to unfold, miracles to witness, hardships to overcome, fears to stare down, people and animals to meet—life in its full range of experience. We can sense much of this inside too, but it is recalled more deeply, felt more intensely, when we get out.

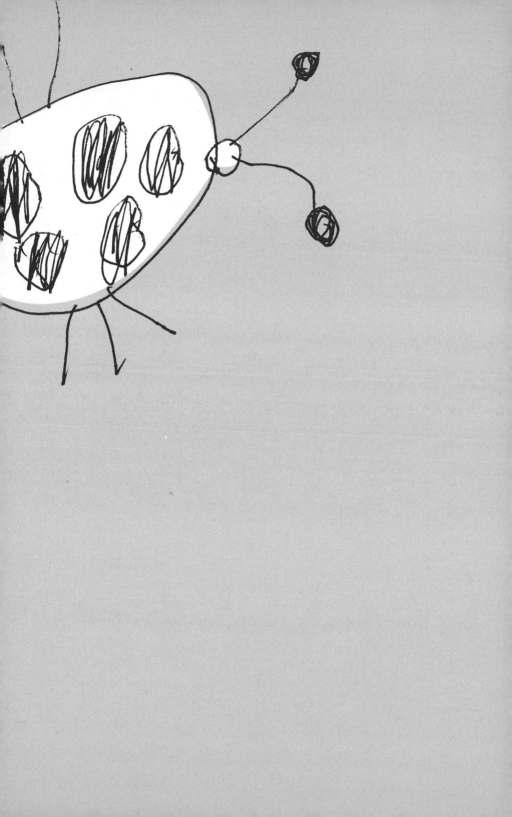

notes

PROLOGUE

xiv   *But the purpose of such collecting is not merely to ac-*
quire   "Eventually," writes Stephen Trimble, "discovery suffices for
power; observation serves as possession." Gary Paul Nabhan and
Stephen Trimble, *The Geography of Childhood: Why Children Need
Wild Places* (Boston: Beacon, 1994), 26.

xv   *a sense of wonder so indestructible that it would last throughout
life . . . the alienation from the sources of our strength*   Rachel Carson, *The Sense of Wonder* (1956; reprint, New York: Harper, 1965).

WALKING TO SCHOOL

1   *Some unwonted, taught pride . . . explore the neighborhood.*   Annie
Dillard, *Pilgrim at Tinker Creek* (1974; reprint, New York: Harper,
1988), 11–12.

5   *loading the ark*   Paul Shepard, "The Ark of the Mind," *Parabola*
8.2 (Summer 1983), 55.

6   *In 1969 half of all children walked or biked . . . half of them make the*
     trip in private cars.   Centers for Disease Control, "Kids Walk-
     to-School: Then and Now—Barriers and Solutions" <www.cdc.
     gov/nccdphp/dnpa/kidswalk/then_and_now.htm>

6   *fear of strangers*   According to the same CDC article, "In 1973 the
     reported rate of violent crimes [calculated by the Bureau of Justice
     Statistics] against children aged 12–19 was approximately 80 cases
     per 1,000 children. Thirty years later, in 2003 the rate has dropped
     to approximately 50 per 1,000 youth."

6   *Stop traffic.*   The National Highway Traffic Safety Administration
     estimates that 20 percent of morning congestion is parents driv-
     ing kids to school. U.S. Department of Transportation, National
     Highway Traffic Safety Administration (NHTSA), "Safe Routes to
     School," 2002 <www.nhtsa.dot.gov/people/injury/pedbimot/bike/
     Safe-Routes-2002>

6   *the kids play only behind fences, on pavement, or on formal play-*
     ground equipment.   Judith H. Heerwagen and Gordon H. Orians
     write: "The design of daycare centers, playgrounds, schools,
     homes, and hospitals could benefit enormously from a bet-
     ter understanding of children's play behaviors. Even a cursory
     investigation of schools and playgrounds shows that little has
     changed over the past fifty years. Children still sit in desks fac-
     ing a teacher or sometimes in clusters of desks. And they play
     in environments dominated by swings and slides or other fixed
     play equipment that does little to capture their imagination." In
     Children and Nature: Psychological, Sociocultural, and Evolutionary
     Investigations, ed. Peter H. Kahn Jr. and Stephen R. Kellert (Cam-
     bridge: MIT Press, 2002), 52.

7   *From ages six to twelve, middle childhood*   See Stephen R. Kellert,
     "Experiencing Nature: Affective, Cognitive, and Evaluative Devel-
     opment in Children," in *Children and Nature*, 133. See also David
     Sobel, *Children's Special Places: Exploring the Role of Forts, Dens,*

and Bush Houses in Middle Childhood (1993; reprint, Detroit: Wayne State Univ. Press, 2002). "The roots of the adult notion of a sense of place are established during middle childhood. Rachel Carson's sense of wonder of early childhood gets transmuted in middle childhood to a sense of exploration. Children leave the security of home behind and set out . . . to discover the new world" (159).

7   *a celebration out here*   Peter Verbeek and Frans B. M. de Waal write in "The Primate Relationship with Nature" that "Finding plentiful food, for instance, has been shown to evoke strong emotional reactions and mediate reciprocity in chimpanzees. A foraging party that discovers an abundant food source may respond by hooting and drumming on trees" (*Children and Nature*, 13).

8   *kept us alive*   Judith H. Heerwagen and Gordon H. Orians note that "The neural process that guided our ancestors' behaviors in Pleistocene hunting and gathering bands are likely to still be in operation today. These mechanisms have been designed by evolution to guide adaptive responses to enduring ecological challenges—such as distinguishing edible from inedible foods, avoiding encounters with dangerous animals, avoiding dangerous conspecifics [animals of the same species], finding the way home, avoiding inanimate hazards, and finding a place to live" ("The Ecological World of Children," in *Children and Nature*, 35).

THE PLACES I'VE LIVED, AND THE ONES I LIVE FOR

15   *except for Abbey*   Abbey married five times and had five children. He spent his first year in the famous Arches trailer the year his first son, Josh, was born.

BEAUTIFUL SCAVENGERS

20   *BANG, went the guns; the birds settled down to sleep. . . . YIKE OUCH HELP went the [distress] recordings; snore went the birds.*   Dillard, *Pilgrim at Tinker Creek*, 37.

20   The *New York Times* story is from August 6, 2003.

20   *local paper that people were worried about pets, disease, and children*   Cover story, "New River Valley Current," *Roanoke Times*, November 14, 2003.

21   *sentimental cloak*   Paul Shepard, "The Mental Menagerie," in *A Paul Shepard Reader: The Only World We've Got* (San Francisco: Sierra Club, 1996), 89.

22   *"important to* know *as to* feel"   Carson, *The Sense of Wonder*, 47.

24   *The Dead Man at Grandview Point*   Edward Abbey, *Desert Solitaire* (1986; reprint, New York: Touchstone, 1990), 215–16.

24   *Vultures*   Mary Oliver, *An American Primitive* (Boston: Little, Brown, 1983), 37–38.

25   *bits of ash in an updraft*   Cormac McCarthy, *The Border Trilogy: All the Pretty Horses, The Crossing, Cities of the Plain* (New York: Everyman's Library, 1999), 707.

SCORCHED EARTH

28   *sorcerers*   Jim Wayne Miller, "Living with Children," in *The Mountains Have Come Home Closer* (Boone, N.C.: Appalachian Consortium Press, 1980), 9.

28   *books, bats, balls, dolls and teddy bears*   Miller, "Saturday Morning," 3.

34   *you must be born again*   Miller, "Born Again," 37.

SKATING POND

41   *This December to February was the warmest on record.*   "U.S. Winter Temperature Near Average: Global December–February Temperature Warmest on Record" <www.ncdc.noaa.gov/oa/climate/research/2007/feb/feb07.htm>. January 2006 was 8.5 degrees above the average daily temperature, according to the National

Climatic Data Center <www.noaanews.noaa.gov/stories2006/ s2576.htm>

41 *Between 1995 and 2005 the average date on the same pond was March 13.* Thoreau gives his ice-out dates in the chapter "Spring" in *Walden.* Journey North students have collected this data:

1995   March 18

1996   March 23

1997   February 22

1998   February 26

1999   March 1

2000   March 9

2001   April 12

2002   February 23

2003   April 2

2004   March 21

2005   April 5

41 *Of the more than 20 species of orchids seen in Concord by Thoreau in the 1850s, for example, only 4 remain today.* Conservation botanist Richard Primack is comparing what's left today to what naturalists such as Thoreau wrote about. *Plant Talk,* January 2005, 5.

41 *Plants now flower about three weeks earlier.* Richard Higgins, "Seasonal Drift Since Thoreau's Time," *Sanctuary: The Journal of the Massachusetts Audubon Society,* Spring 2005, 6–9.

42 *They who dwell near the river hear the ice crack . . . as if its icy fetters were rent from end to end.* Thoreau, "Spring," *Walden.*

43 *Young men of the area caught a train to Belspring and skated back to Radford along almost fifteen miles of the twisting river. Radford Then and Now: A Pictorial History* (Radford, Va.: American Bicentennial History, 1975), 27.

43 *indoor skiing* See <www.skidubai.com>. Synthetic skating surfaces are also real: <www.coldproducts.com/ezglide.php>

45 *Children, especially, are intrigued . . . . unspoiled sense of wonder* Euell Gibbons, *Stalking the Wild Asparagus* (Putney, Vt.: Alan
C. Hood, 1962), 2–3.

46 *unfenced Nature reaching up to your very sills* Thoreau, "Sounds,"
Walden.

46 *lawnmowers emitted ninety-three times more smog-forming pollutants per gallon than emitted that same year's cars* Felicity Bar-
ringer, "A Greener Way to Cut the Grass Runs Afoul of a Powerful
Lobby," *New York Times*, April 24, 2006.

46 *ten times more chemicals per acre than farmers* "Homeowners
Guide to Protecting Frogs," U.S. Fish and Wildlife Service
<www.fws.gov/contaminants/Documents/Homeowners_Guide_
Frogs.pdf>

47 *the country of wide lawns* F. Scott Fitzgerald, *The Great Gatsby*
(1925; reprint, New York: Scribner, 2000), 21.

47 *started at the beach and ran toward the front door for a quarter of
a mile, jumping over sun-dials and brick walls and burning gardens* Fitzgerald, *Great Gatsby*, 23.

47 *I want to get the grass cut* Fitzgerald, *Great Gatsby*, 80.

47 *"blue lawn" that "he had come a long way to"* Fitzgerald, *Great
Gatsby*, 154.

48 *moral character and social responsibility with the condition of
the lawn* Paul Robbins and Julie Sharp, "The Lawn-Chemical
Economy and Its Discontents," *Antipode* 35 (November 2003), 962.

50 *Eaten with pot roast and gravy, one of my favorite vegetables* Gibbons, *Stalking the Wild Asparagus*, 133.

51 *waged a one-man war against weeds* Ted Steinberg, *American
Green: The Obsessive Quest for the Perfect Lawn* (New York: Norton,
2006), 40.

51 *Dr. Spock of yard care* Steinberg, *American Green*, 42.

51 *Robert Sapolsky*   *All Things Considered*, National Public Radio, August 15, 2006.

53 *Lilliputian landscape*   Nabhan and Trimble, *The Geography of Childhood*, 4. "I've come to realize that a few intimate places mean more to my children, and to others, than all the glorious panoramas I could ever show them" (7).

54 *so closely resemble asparagus some may be fooled*   Gibbons, *Stalking the Wild Asparagus*, 174.

54 *"commensurate" to their "capacity to wonder"*   Fitzgerald, *Great Gatsby*, 154.

CREEK WALKING

58 *Almost half of all Virginia waterways are not fit to play or swim in.*   "2006 Water Quality Assessment Report," Virginia Department of Environmental Quality <www.deq.virginia.gov/wqa/305b2006.html>. We have only recently learned that the New River and its tributaries host their own species of crayfish, the New River crayfish, *Cambarus sciotensis*, but we have not caught Big Daddy since to verify. His claw will lack tubercles and rough areas. New River crayfish have smooth hands.

60 *Paddle to the Sea*   Based on the Holling C. Holling book.

HOLY LAND

65 *Assume you are willing . . . the best one there is.*   Maurice Brooks, *The Appalachians* (Boston: Houghton Mifflin, 1965), 246.

69 *neatly showing how isolation is a force for the evolution of new species* and *islands in the sky*   Scott Weidensaul, *Mountains of the Heart: A Natural History of the Appalachians* (Golden, Colo.: Fulcrum, 1994), 39.

71 *patron saint to the entire family of Plethodontidae*   Brooks, *The Appalachians*, 254.

72   *not a whit more warmed by Zenobia's passion, than a salamander by its native furnace*   Nathaniel Hawthorne, *The Blithedale Romance* (New York: Bedford / St. Martin's, 1996), 113.

72   *Let me enter a tract of rich forest . . . world hidden beneath* and *giants of the microcosm*   Edward O. Wilson, *The Future of Life* (New York: Knopf, 2002), xv–xvi.

BRIDGE 33

78   *all the old feeling*   Ernest Hemingway, "Big Two Hearted River, Part I," in *In Our Time* (1925; reprint, New York: Scribner's, 1970), 134.

FIELD GUIDES

82   *He needs the companionship of at least one adult who can share it, rediscovering with him the joy, excitement, and mystery of the world we live in.*   Carson, *The Sense of Wonder*, 45.

90   *Attention is the beginning of devotion.*   Mary Oliver, "Upstream," *Orion*, May/June 2004, 59.

91   *Imagine if they knew plants and animals the way they knew brand names and logos.*   David Orr writes that "We know, too, that young people on average can recognize over 1,000 corporate logos but only a handful of plants and animals native to their places" ("Political Economy and the Ecology of Childhood," *Children and Nature*, 282).

SWIMMING HOLE

92   *the cleanest mainstem river in Virginia.*   A relative distinction. All the rivers (Potomac, Shenandoah, Rappahannock, Roanoke, York) are "impaired" in some way or another. The Department of Environmental Quality (DEQ) has found dangerous levels of PCBS

in the tissue of bottom feeders like carp and catfish on the Radford
section, causing them to issue a fish consumption advisory. It has
also found DDT (a pesticide), mercury, and heptachlor (insecticide)
in fish.

93   *cutting themselves off from the pain*   David Sobel, *Ecophobia:
Reclaiming the Heart in Nature Education* (Great Barrington, Mass.:
Orion, 1996), 2.

93   *modeling by a responsible adult*   Sobel, *Ecophobia*, 10.

94   *Deranged Otter Attacks Pregnant Woman*   Shawna Morrison, "Otter Attack Creates Creature Discomfort," *Roanoke Times*, August 28,
2006, A-1.

95   *River of Death*   Patricia Givens Johnson, *New River Early Settlement* (Pulaski, Va.: Edmonds, 1983).

96   *designed to accommodate recreational needs and activities downstream from the dam on New River*   AEP <www.appalachianpower.
com/news/releases>

96   *website of real-time data*   USGS <http://waterdata.usgs.gov/usa/
nwis/uv?site_no=03171000>

96   *a consistent 1,730 feet about sea level*   From data provided by
Theresa Rogers, a supervisor at American Electric Power.

98   *swimminghole.org*   "Swimming Holes.info." Maintained by Tom
Hillegrass and Dave Hajdasz (2005).

101   *A "dunkard" was a term of derision for people who were "dunkers,"
German Baptists who practiced a trine (as in Trinity) immersion
baptism.*   Paul Schach, "Comments on Some Pennsylvania-Ger-
man Words in the Dictionary of Americanisms," *American Speech*
29.1 (Feb. 1954), 45–54.

102   *founded on the premise that their waters . . . could cure common
diseases at a time when medical science really could not do much
for patients*   Stan Cohen, *Historic Springs of the Virginias: A Pictorial History* (1981; reprint, Charleston, W.V.: Pictorial Histories,
1997), vii.

114 *For special places to work their magic on kids. . . . They need to be free to climb trees.* Robert Michael Pyle, "Eden in a Vacant Lot," in *Children and Nature*, 319.

118 *children feel a deep urge to move into the larger world away from home to find a place for themselves.* Sobel, *Children's Special Places*, 108. The rest of the paragraph is from his close (160–61).

119 *"creeping through that pitch-dark tunnel," listening to the "singing in my ears"* Vladimir Nabokov, *Speak, Memory: An Autobiography Revisited* (1960; reprint, New York: Putnam, 1966), 23.

120 *safe up there from jackals' visits during the night* Johann Whyss, *The Swiss Family Robinson* (New York: World Publishing Company, 1947), 62–63.

124 *thirty-five hours of screen time per week* That figure comes from the Executive Summary of a Kaiser Family Foundation report. "Generation M: Media in the Lives of 8 to 18 Year-Olds," March 9, 2005 <www.kff.org/entmedia/entmedia030905pkg.cfm>, accessed October 25, 2006.

125 *two little feet* I am thinking here of singer Greg Brown: "two little feet to get me 'cross the mountain / two little feet to carry me away into the woods / . . . / tumble us like scree let us holler out our freedom like a / like a wolf across a valley like a kid lost in a game / no time no name gonna miss that plane again" (Hacklebarney Music, 1996).

126 *inner cadence that brings fruit to ripeness* Sam Keen, *Hymns to an Unknown God* (New York: Bantam, 1994), 266.

127 *shine like jewels . . . lives* Louise Chawla, "Ecstatic Places," *Children's Environmental Quarterly* 7.4 (Winter 1986), 23.

127 *meaningful images . . . nature* Chawla, "Ecstatic Places," 23.

129   *spectacle of life . . . prelude*   Rachel Carson, *The Edge of the Sea*
       (New York: Houghton Mifflin, 1955), 7

130   *her biographer*   Linda Lear, *Rachel Carson: Witness for Nature*
       (New York: Henry Holt, 1997), 4

130   *comes to my door without half trying*   Quoted in Lear, *Rachel Car-
       son*, 348.

130   Letter to Dorothy Freeman from *Always Rachel: The Letters of
       Rachel Carson and Dorothy Freeman, 1952–1964* (Boston: Beacon,
       1995), 490.

130ff Carson's notes all from Rachel Carson Papers, Yale Collection of
       American Literature, Beinecke Rare Book and Manuscript Library,
       Yale University.

131   *sand-colored, fleet-legged beings*   Carson, *The Sense of Wonder*, 10.

131   *alone with the sea*   Carson, *The Sense of Wonder*, 5.

132   *sight of these . . . overtones*   Carson, *The Sense of Wonder*, 10.

136   *Lilliputian beings . . . grains of sand*   Carson, *The Edge of the Sea*, 2.

138   *fairy cave . . . fairy pool*   Carson, *The Edge of the Sea*, 2–4.

138   *We have let him . . . mica embedded in them.*   Carson, *The Sense of
       Wonder*, 22.

143   *To attract sugaring moths*   See Elizabeth Lawlor, *Discover Nature at
       Sundown* (Stackpole, 1995), for more on sugaring moths and other
       nighttime creatures (113). The whole *Discover Nature* series is a
       great resource.

144   *I used to spend hours in the backyard . . . littering the grass with dried
       lappets and strips.*   Dillard, *Pilgrim at Tinker Creek*, 88.

144   *They need the organized, linear play but also the creative, lateral
       kind.*   An American Academy of Pediatrics (AAP) report stresses
       that "free and unstructured play is healthy and—in fact—essential

for helping children reach important social, emotional, and cognitive developmental milestones as well as helping them manage stress and become resilient." November 11, 2006 <www.aap.org/pressroom/play-public.htm>

148 *Americans spend an estimated 90 percent of their time indoors and have higher exposures to indoor allergens.* "About Asthma," EPA <www.epa.gov/asthma/about.html>

148 *Outside lies magic.* John R. Stilgoe, *Outside Lies Magic: Regaining History and Awareness in Everyday Places* (New York: Walker, 1999).

acknowl-
edgments

THANKS TO RADFORD UNIVERSITY for a professional leave to devote time to writing—and child rearing. Thanks to Jim Minick for playing "tradesies"—I only hope my comments were as valuable to him as his were to me. Thanks to Tim Poland for his comments and for his wise counsel about how to spend that leave. Thanks to Clyde Kessler and Rudi Woykowski for getting us into the field. Thanks to Frank Taylor, Bob Sheehy, Paul Angermeier, Jim Fraser, Keith Bildstein, James Organ, and Kevin Hahmed for talking with me about the life sciences. Thanks to Steve Keighton for answering questions meteorological.

Thanks to Trev Smith and Jenny Schwenke for their "happy hollow," and to Harry Groot for his wood. And thanks to all the kids who came along: Noah Solomon, Sarah Kern, Finn McKinley, Bethany Pierce, Cameron Schafer, Max and Eli Lawrence, Lindsey and Lucas Mathews, and Mrs. Arthur's second-grade class. Thanks to readers for their forbearance. Thanks to Mook for fifteen fantastic years.

Thanks to Bill Kovarik of *Appalachian Voices* and Terry Lee of *Double Take / Points of Entry* for publishing "Beautiful Scavengers," and thanks to

Julie Dunlap for including "Scorched Earth" in *Companions to Wonder.* Thanks to Nick Neely and *Watershed* for their work with "Weed Eaters." Thanks to Mark Taylor and the *Roanoke Times* for publishing "Nordic Fun" (www.roanoke.com). Thanks to Charlie Waters and Chip Chase of Whitegrass for having fun.

Reprinted by permission of Frances Collin, Trustee: Excerpts from *The Edge of the Sea* by Rachel Carson, copyright © 1955 by Rachel L. Carson. Excerpts from *Always, Rachel: The Letters of Rachel Carson and Dorothy Freeman, 1952–1964*, copyright © 1995 by Roger Allen Christie. Excerpts from *Rachel Carson: Witness for Nature* by Linda Lear, copyright © 1997 by Linda Lear. Excerpts from *The Sense of Wonder*, copyright © 1956 by Rachel L. Carson. Excerpts from unpublished Rachel Carson material copyright © by Roger A. Christie.

Thanks to the Beinecke Rare Book and Manuscript Library at Yale University for access to Carson's papers and to the Frances Collin Literary Agency for permission to publish them. Thanks to Judy Purdy and the staff of the University of Georgia Press for making this look and sound better. Aaron Hill is an awesome artist, and mom Mindy isn't a bad designer herself—thanks to you both. Thanks to Daniel Simon for improving the way it reads.

Thanks to Dr. Jane Vogel for her comment in eleventh grade. I guess I am going to be a writer. Thanks to Bill Roorbach for getting me back "into woods." Thanks to singer Greg Brown. Thanks to my parents for planting the seeds that have sprouted here.

"More than any other human relationship, overwhelmingly more," wrote Tillie Olsen in *Silences*, "[parenthood] means being instantly interruptible." Thanks especially to Sam and Elliot for time to write and even for the interruptions, which, after all, are the subject of this book. And thanks to my wife, Catherine, for making it all possible. No other comments in the making of this book have been more consequential, nor more tenderly put forward.